AALTO: 10 Selected Houses

First published in Japan on March 31, 2008
Seventh published on September 30, 2021
TOTO Publishing (TOTO LTD,)   TOTO Nogizaka Bldg. 2F
1-24-3, Minami-Aoyama,
Minato-ku, Tokyo 107-0062, Japan
[Sales] TEL: +81-3-3402-7138 FAX: +81-3-3402-7187
[Editorial] TEL: +81-3-3497-1010
[URL] https://jp.toto.com/publishing

Copyright ───────────── © 2008 Yutaka Saito
Photographs copyright ───── © 2008 Yutaka Saito
Drawings & monochrome
photographs copyright ───── © 2008 Alvar Aalto Foundation

Author ──────────── Yutaka Saito
Publisher ─────────── Takeshi Ito
Editor ───────────── Naomi Miwa
Book Design ───────── Ryohei Kojima, Ryota Kojima
Printer ──────────── TOSHO Printing Co., Ltd.

ISBN978-4-88706-290-0

AALTO

10 Selected Houses │ アールトの住宅

齋藤 裕

by Yutaka Saito

TOTO出版

Book Design：Ryohei Kojima

AALTO

10 Selected Houses アールトの住宅

目次
Contents

アルヴァ・アールト Alvar Aalto

1898
2月3日、フィンランドのクオルターネに生まれる
Born on February 3 in Kuortane, Finland.

1903
ユヴァスキラに移る
The Aalto family moved to Jyväskylä.

1916
ヘルシンキ工科大学で建築を学ぶ
Studied architecture at Helsinki University of Technology (–1921).

1923
建築事務所をユヴァスキラに開設
Opened office in Jyväskylä.

1924
建築家のアイノ・マルシオと結婚
Married architect Aino Marsio.

1927
トゥルクへ事務所を移す
Moved office to Turku.

1929
フランクフルトで開かれた第2回CIAM(近代建築国際会議)に参加
Attended the 2nd Congrès Internationaux d'Architecture Moderne (CIAM) in Frankfurt.

1930
ブリュッセルで第3回CIAMに参加
Attended the 3rd CIAM conference in Brussels.

1933
ヘルシンキへ事務所を移す
アテネで第4回CIAMに参加
Moved office to Helsinki.
Attended the 4th CIAM conference in Athens.

1935
アールトの家具を販売するアルテック社を設立
アムステルダムで第6回CIAMに参加
Founded the Artek Company to distribute Aalto's furniture and glassware.
Attended the 6th CIAM conference in Amsterdam.

1938
ニューヨーク近代美術館で展覧会「アルヴァ・アールトの建築と家具」を開催
Exhibition, *Alvar Aalto: Architecture and Furniture*, Museum of Modern Art, New York.

1940
マサチューセッツ工科大学で研究教授に任命される
ヨーロッパの戦争激化のため帰国
Research Professor at Massachusetts Institute of Technology, Cambridge, USA.
Returned to Finland due to the aggravation of war in Europe.

1946
マサチューセッツ工科大学で客員教授を務める
Visiting Professor at Massachusetts Institute of Technology (–1948).

1949
1月13日、妻のアイノ・アールト死去
Aino Aalto died on January 13.

1952
建築家のエルサ(エリッサ)・マキニエミと結婚
Married architect Elsa (Elissa) Mäkiniemi.

1957
王立英国建築家協会よりゴールド・メダルを受賞
Awarded the Gold Medal by the Royal Institute of British Architects.

1963
アメリカ建築家協会よりゴールド・メダルを受賞
Awarded the Gold Medal by the American Institute of Architects.

1965
フィレンツェのストロッツィ宮殿で回顧展
Retrospective exhibition, Palazzo Strozzi, Florence, Italy.

1972
フランス建築アカデミーよりゴールド・メダルを受賞
Awarded the Gold Medal by the French Academy of Architecture.

1976
5月11日、ヘルシンキで死去
Died in Helsinki on May 11.

Aalto Summer House   1952-53

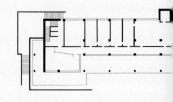

Helsinki University of Technology   1953-66

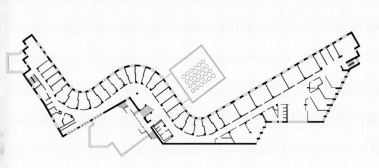

Baker House, Senior Dormintory for MIT   1946-49

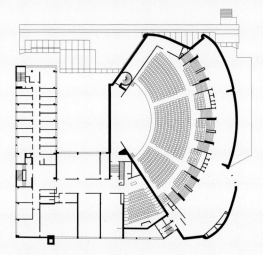

House of Culture   1952-58

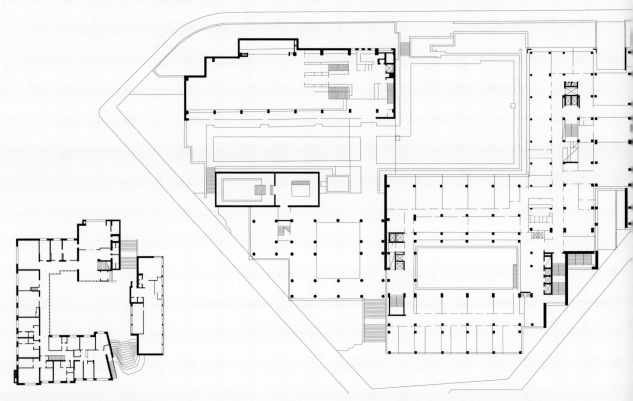

Säynätsalo Town Hall   1948-52

National Pensions Institute   1953-57

主要作品プラン

アルヴァ・アールトの建築家としての歩みは、事務所を開設した1923年から亡くなる1976年まで50余年にわたる。スエーデンの建築家アスプルンドに私淑した20代、機能主義の洗礼を受け、建築やアート分野でモダニストたちとの国際的な交流を築いた30代、そして、最初の黄金時代を迎えつつあった40代には第二次世界大戦が勃発する。戦後の40代後半からは、疲弊したフィンランドの復興と近代化に貢献すべく、大学や行政機関の建物、都市や企業のマスタープランづくりなど、大規模でモニュメンタルなプロジェクトを手がけた。不動の地位を築いた最晩年にかけては、海外からも文化施設などの依頼を多く受けている。

そんなアールトの軌跡を、本書で紹介した個人住宅10件を含めて、プランを時系列に並べて俯瞰しようとしたのがこの表である。戦前（グレー線より左）は、アスプルンドやバウハウスの影響を受けながらも自己の表現を見いだそうとしていた、アールトのいわば「実験時代」である。戦後は、中庭を核とするプログラムの組みたてや、グー・チョキ・パーのような独特のフィンガーフォーム・プランを応用・展開し、小さな個人住宅であっても大きな公共建築であっても、これらはアールトが温め、深めていった根本的なデザイン・モティーフであったのが見えてくる。

晩年のいくつかのプロジェクトについては、設計からかなり時間を経て建設されており、それらについては設計期間を示すのみとした。縮尺は1/1000に統一している。

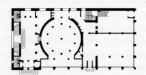

Jyväskylä Workers' Club   1924-25

Villa Tammekann   1932-33

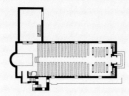

Muurame Church   1926-29

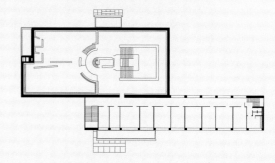

Viipuri City Library   1933-35

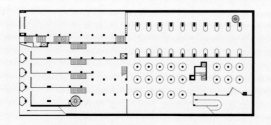

Turun Sanomat Building   1928-30

Paimio Tuberculosis Sanatorium   1929-32

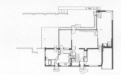

Aalto House & Studio   1935-36

Villa Mairea   1937-39

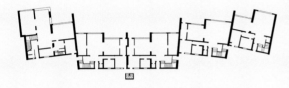

Housing for Sunila Pulp Mill   1936-38

Finnish Pavilion for New York World's Fair   1938-39

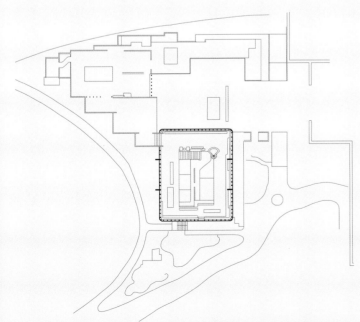

Finnish Pavilion for Paris World's Fair   1936-37

見学可能なアールトの住宅作品
Aalto Designed Houses Open to the Public

メゾン・カレ　Maison Carré

2 chemin du Saint-Sacrement, 78490 Bazoches-sur-Guyonne, France

Information available at http://www.maisonlouiscarre.fr/

Email at resa@maisonlouiscarre.fr

Tel +33 (0)1 34 86 79 63

アールト自邸とスタジオ　Aalto House & Studio

Riihitie 20, 00330 Helsinki, Finland

Information available at http://www.alvaraalto.fi/info/guide/helsinki.htm

Email at riihitie@alvaraalto.fi

アールト夏の家　Aalto Summer House on Muuratsalo Island

Information available at http://www.alvaraalto.fi/info/guide/jyvaskyla.htm

Email at museum@alvaraalto.fi

Tel +358 (0)14 266 7113 (Alvar Aalto Museum)

ヴィラ・マイレア　Villa Mairea

Pikkukoivukuja 20, 29 600 Noormarkku, Finland

Information available at www.villamairea.fi/

Email at info@villamairea.fi

Tel +358 (0)10 888 44 60

ヴィラ・コッコネン　Villa Kokkonen

Tuulimyllyntie 5, 04400 Järvenpää, Finland

Information available at www.villakokkonen.fi

Email at info@villakokkonen.fi

ヴィラ・タンメカン　Villa Tammekann

F. R. kreutzwaldi 6, Tartu, Estonia

The Granö Center of the Universities of Turku and Tartu

Information available at http://granokeskus.utu.fi/

* 個人所有の住宅は除く

* その他の作品についての情報 http://www.alvaraalto.fi/

* The privately owned houses are excluded from the list above.

* More information on Aalto's other works is available at http://www.alvaraalto.fi/

RUSSIA

SWEDEN

Gulf of Bothnia

FINLAND

Rovaniemi

Jyväskylä

Seinäjoki

Muurame ● Säynätsalo
Korpilahti ● Muuratsalo

Noormarkku

Imatra

● Vyborg

Summa

Järvenpää

Paimio

Turku

Kotka

St.Petersburg ●

Tammisaari

Helsinki

Gulf of Finland

NORWAY

Stockholm

Tallinn

ESTONIA

Tartu

メゾン・カレ

Maison Carré

Bazoches-sur-Guyonne, France (1956 —1959)

林のなか、蛇行するアプローチを登る
The approach winds upward through a grove.

緑のなかの白い斜線。明快な屋根のコンセプト
A white wall emerges through the greenery, setting off the sharp diagonal of the roof.

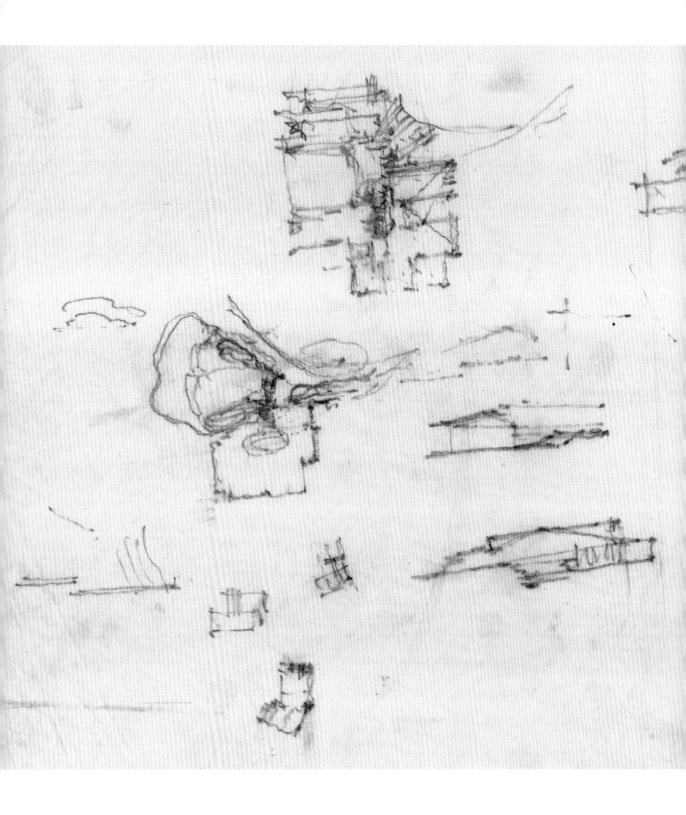

初期のスケッチ。プランのゾーニングを西向きと南向きで二つのヴォリュームに分ける案をスタディ。一つは玄関ホールとリビングルーム、もう一つは個室を含むプライベート・ゾーンである。この段階でリビングルームは西向き、ベッドルームは南向きと決めている。また、丘陵の勾配を利用してスキップフロアにしようと考えている

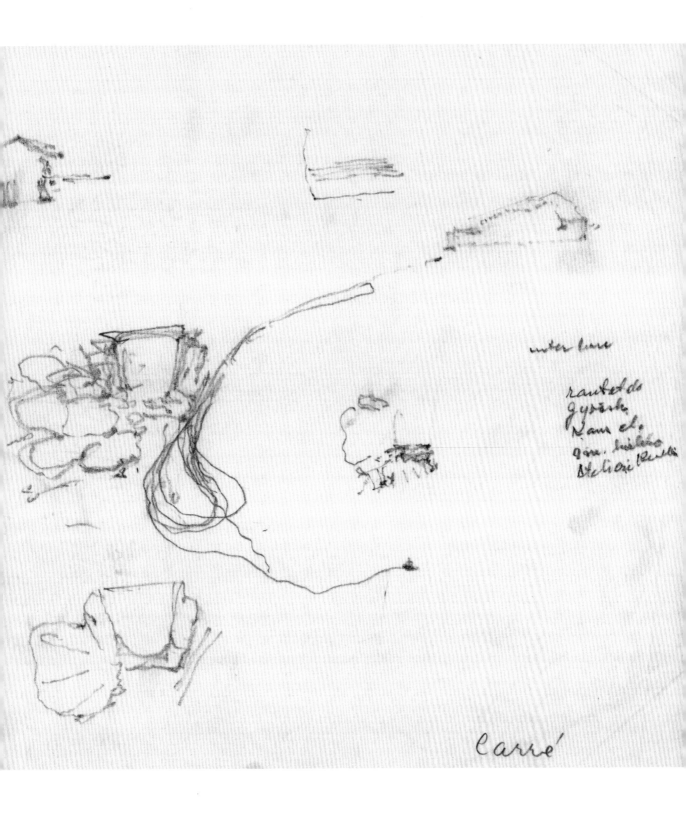

Carré

Initial sketches show Aalto's study for dividing the plan into two volumes for different living zones facing west and south. One volume is the entrance hall and living room; the other is the private zone with the bedrooms. At this stage, he has the living room facing west and the bedrooms facing south. He planned to use the slope of the hill to make the house split-level.

西側エレベーションのスケッチ。斜め俯瞰から見たときの屋根をスタディする。屋根のあり方はこの住宅の着想の主眼点。出っ張ったり引っこんだり、かなり複雑な形をイメージしている。リビングの煙突や奥に見えるかもしれないキッチンの煙突、前面の植栽の量感まで想定して描きこんである

The sketches of the west elevation show a study from a view looking down on the roof from an angle. The idea for the roof is the main feature of the design for this house. With its projections and indentations, it evokes quite a complex shape. We can see how the sketches take into account not only the living room chimney and the way the kitchen chimney will be seen but also the volume of the shrubbery in front of the living room.

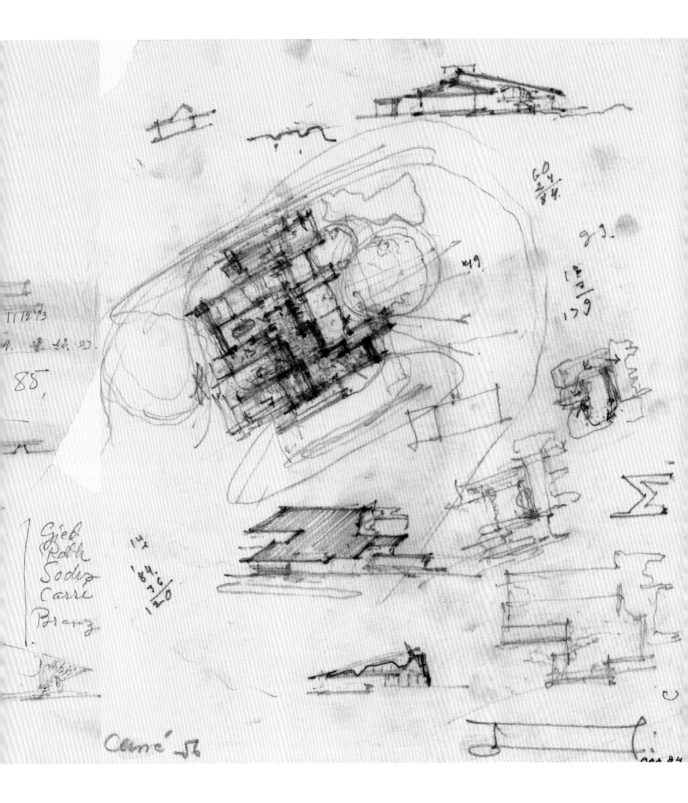

中央にプランスケッチがあり、3、6、7の数字は部屋の幅を表わす。各部屋の大きさや配置はすでにできあがっている。右端にはまわる動線を矢印で示したメモ。玄関ホールの波状の天井と屋根のスケッチがあるが、実現した空間と絵のプロポーションはほとんど変わらない

In the plan sketch in the middle, the numbers 3, 6, and 7 stand for the width of the rooms. The size and layout of the rooms are already established. At the right side is a memo with the lines of movement indicated by arrows. At the bottom there is also a sketch of the undulations of the entrance hall ceiling, and at the top a sketch of the roof. Remarkably, the space as finally realized and the proportions suggested in the sketches are almost identical.

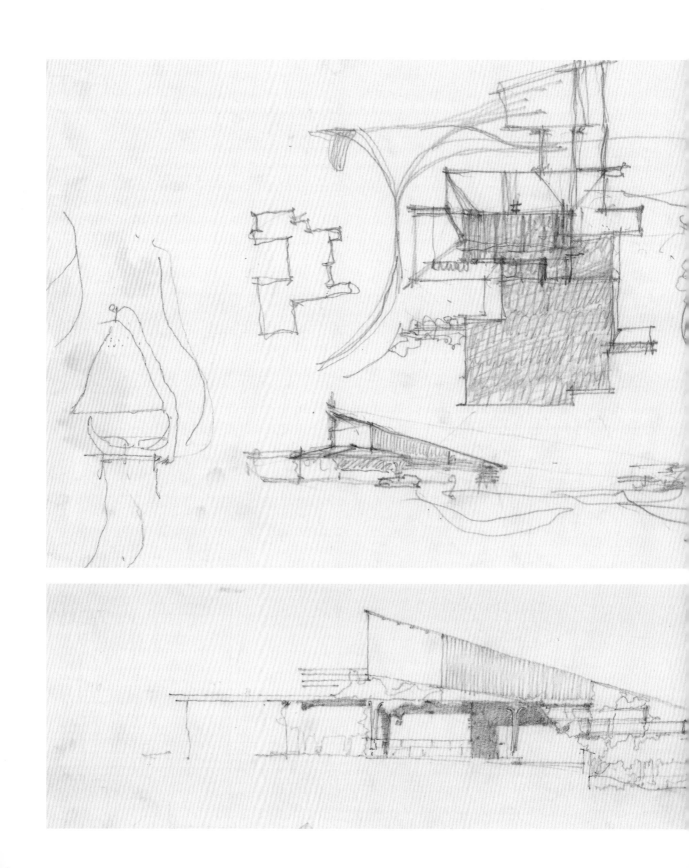

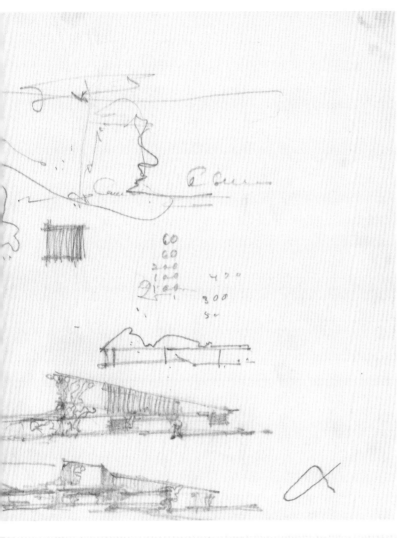

上は屋根伏図。東側に車庫の屋根を連結したらどうなるかをスタディしている。その下のエレベーション・スケッチでは、車庫を連結したときのファサードの見え方を想定。下図も同じ。片流れ屋根の高い方の側面に水平の要素を加えて全体のバランスを取ることを考えている。最終案では、車庫は母屋と離して別棟にした

Roof plan sketch at the top, with a study showing the addition of a garage on the east side. The elevation sketches below, including the large one, are projections of the facade with the garage added. A horizontal element is added at the high end of the inclined roof in order to improve the balance of the whole. In the final stage, the garage was made a separate structure from the main house.

北側、正面ファサード。夕方近くの光
North side, with front facade, in nearly evening light.

玄関。軽快な庇とスタイリッシュな柱の組みあわせ。腰壁はシャルトル産ライムストーン、木部はチーク、鉄柱にはコンクリートを充填してある

Entrance. The lower part of the wall is Chartres limestone, the woodwork is teak, and the steel post is filled with concrete.

太陽が沈む頃、西日に照らされる北西面。木々や芝の緑は暗くなり、明暗のコントラストが強まる時間

At sunset, the western sun lights up the northwestern side of the house. Caught at a moment when the light brings out the contrast of light and dark, the house comes aglow against the darkened woods and lawn.

室内の照明と外の光が融けあうような日暮れのひととき。太陽は森の向こうに沈み、
雲に反射した夕日が庇の奥に入りこむ

At that brief evening moment when interior illumination mingles with external
light, the glow reflected off the clouds from the sun, already sunk beyond the
woods, enters deep beneath the eaves.

(左) 三角形の白壁と石壁との間に窓を取る。窓の高さに合わせて、軒下に切りこみを入れた美しいディテール
(上) 緊張感のある壁と軒天井の収まり

(Left) A window is positioned between the white of the triangular upper wall and the limestone of the lower wall. Note the indentation of the eaves cleanly aligned with the height of the window.
(Above) The wall and ceiling under the eaves are finished with clean, taut lines.

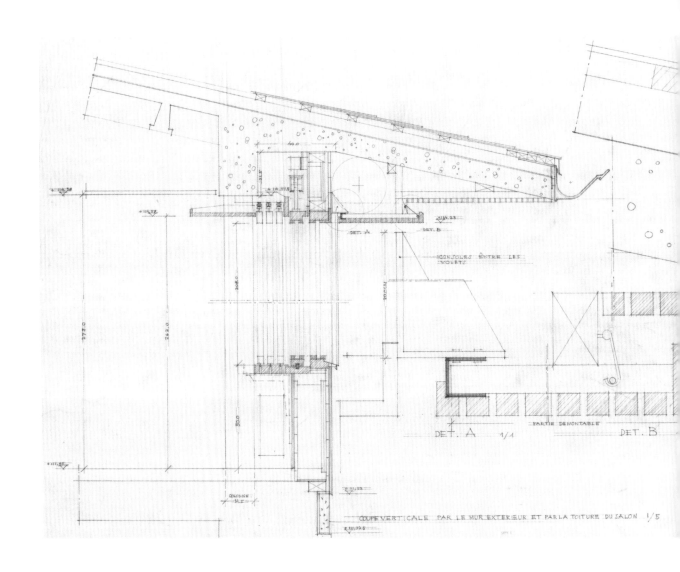

（上）窓、シャッターボックス、雨樋の詳細図。アールトの住宅のなかでもヴィラ・マイレアとメゾン・カレのディテールは、原寸図まで
起こして緻密にデザインを練りあげている
（右）西側の大屋根の雨を受ける樋先。大雨が降ったとき、雨受け皿の中心に水が落下する

(Above) Detail drawings of the shutter box and eaves trough. Among the designs of Aalto's houses, those for the Villa Mairea and
Maison Carré show minutely worked-out full scale drawings.
(Right) Tip of eaves where rain collects from the large main roof on the west side, showing spout and drain positioned to receive
the drainage in a heavy downpour.

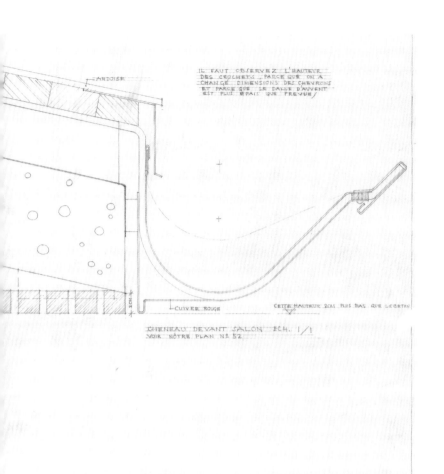

IL FAUT OBSERVEZ L'HAUTEUR
DES CROCHETS, PARCE QUE ON A
CHANGE DIMENSIONS DES CHEVRONS
ET PARCE QUE LE DALLE D'AUVENT
EST PLUS ÉPAIS QUE PREVUE/

— ARDOISE

CUIVRE ROUGE

CETTE HAUTEUR 2CM PLUS BAS QUE L'EGREAN

CHENEAU DEVANT SALON ECH. 1/1
VOIR NÔTRE PLAN № 52

architecte alvar aalto
MAISON DE MONSIEUR CARRÉ
COUPE VERTICALE PARTIE
RUE BUXAGNY
BAZOCHE / GUYON/ S. O. /17.5.58
MODIFIE COMPLETE = 2.5.58

西側。丘の傾斜に呼応した大きなスレート屋根
Western facade. The lines of the expansive slate roof echo the contours of the hill.

白い壁の量感で構成した南側
The south side, showing the combination of white-walled volumes.

東面。大きな三角形の側面をどう見せるか。白壁の量感を刻み、下屋を連結し、窓の配置や形にリズムをつけて巧みにまとめている。上階はスタッフのベッドルームで、下階にはキッチンとスタッフルームがある

Eastern facade. How to design the side of the large triangle? Cutting into the volume of the white wall and connected to the lower part of the house, this part of the design balances the whole with a skillful rhythm in the shape and positioning of the windows. The upper level has housekeepers' rooms and the lower level the kitchen and staff room.

洗練されたディテール処理が随所に散りば
められている。竪樋や通気口（右上）は隠さ
ず、デザイン要素として見せている

Every part of the design shows
extremely refined handling of detail. The
drainpipes and vents (top right) are not
concealed but on display, themselves
elements of the design.

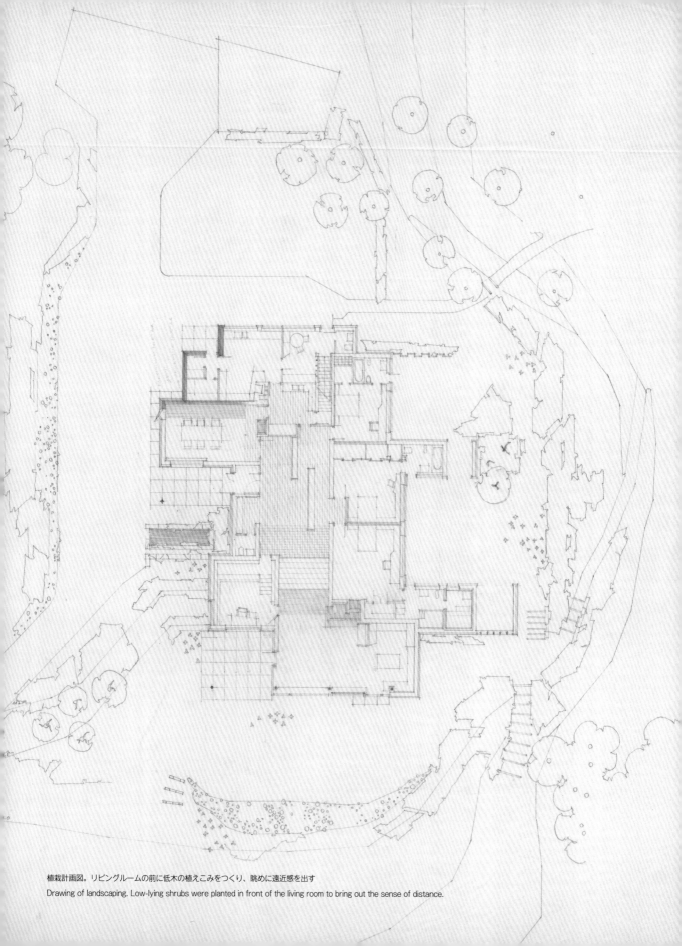

植栽計画図。リビングルームの前に低木の植えこみをつくり、眺めに遠近感を出す

Drawing of landscaping. Low-lying shrubs were planted in front of the living room to bring out the sense of distance.

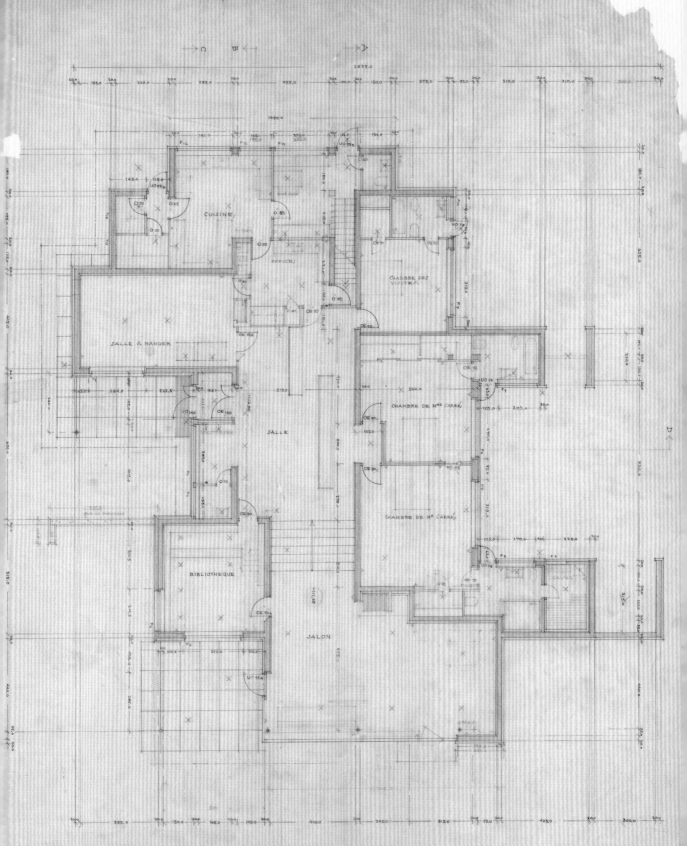

構造体に仕上げやディテールを描きこみ、寸法を明確に示した最終段階の平面図。1957年3月9日付
Final stage floor plan, showing the finishing and details of the structure and giving precise measurements. Dated March 9, 1957.

玄関ホール。内側から膨らむような包容感と開放感を兼ね備えた空間

Entrance hall. As if swelling up from within, this is a space that combines a sense of both embrace and expansiveness.

玄関ホールからリビングルームを見る
View through the entrance hall toward the living room.

(左) 階段を下り、リビングルームへ。庭の眺めを室内いっぱいに取りこむ
(上) 柔らかな曲線のテーブル、精緻な仕上げの天井。洗練されたなかにも温かみある雰囲気は、アールトのインテリアの真髄

(Left) Looking into the living room from the steps down from the entrance hall. The windows open up the view of the garden even from far back in the room.
(Above) The essence of Aalto's interior here is the atmosphere of both refinement and warmth created by gently curving lines of furnishings and precisely finished ceiling woodwork.

リビングルーム。奥には書斎。家具はこの家のためにデザインされたオリジナルのものが残されている
Living room. The study is visible at back right. The furniture, originally designed for this house, has been preserved.

西日の差しこむ春の夕方。天井に高低差をつけ、暖炉まわりの空間の密度を上げる

Western sun shining into the living room on a spring evening. The density of the space around the fireplace is enhanced with varied ceiling heights.

格調高いプロポーションの暖炉。視界にはつねに玄関ホールの存在がある

The proportions of the fireplace are stylish. From whichever way you look, the entrance hall enters the line of vision.

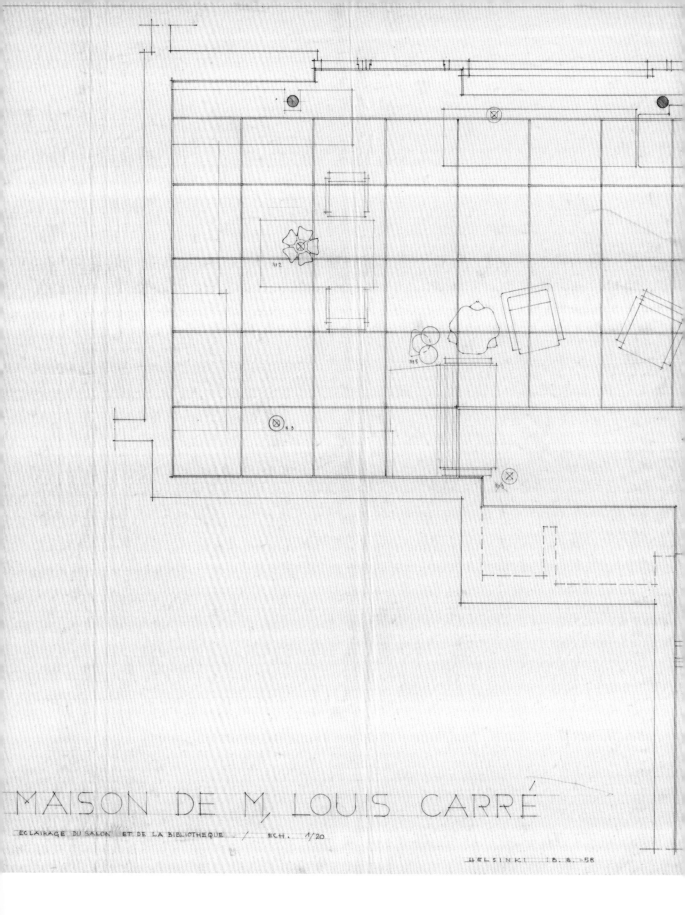

MAISON DE M, LOUIS CARRÉ

ECLAIRAGE DU SALON ET DE LA BIBLIOTHEQUE / ECH. 1/20

HELSINKI 18. 8. -58

74

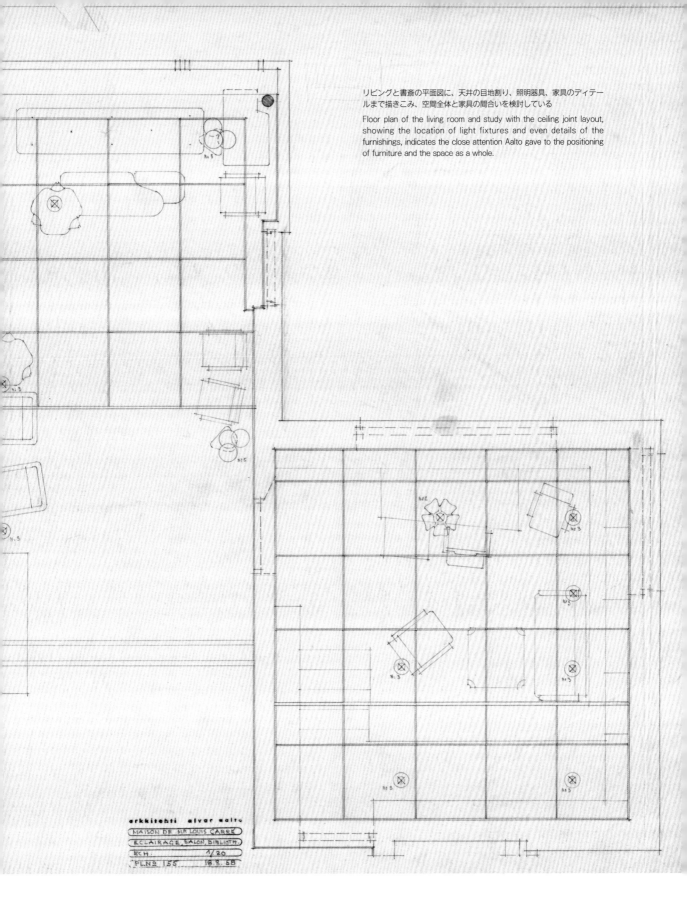

リビングと書斎の平面図に、天井の目地割り、照明器具、家具のディテールまで描きこみ、空間全体と家具の間合いを検討している

Floor plan of the living room and study with the ceiling joint layout, showing the location of light fixtures and even details of the furnishings, indicates the close attention Aalto gave to the positioning of furniture and the space as a whole.

書斎。この部屋はスキップフロアになっていて、右側の床が天井と共に高くなっている

Study. This room has a split-level floor, the elevated part is visible where the ceiling rises on the right.

西に窓を向けたダイニングルーム。照明器具は壁の絵を照らすためにデザインされたもの。奥の壁には風を通すための小窓がついている。
上のモノクロ写真は 1960 年頃に撮影されたもの

Dining room, with west-facing window. The light fixtures were designed to illuminate paintings hung on the walls. The small window at the back is for ventilation. The monochrome image above was taken around 1960 by Heikki Havas.

（上）玄関ホールからカレ氏のベッドルームへ
（下）壁内に暖炉を組みこんだデザイン

(Top) Bedroom of Mr. Carré from the entrance hall.
(Bottom) The interior wall is designed to incorporate a fireplace.

（上）南に窓を取ったカレ氏のベッドルーム
（下）バスルーム、奥にはサウナ。左手前に扉があり、屋
外へ通じる

(Top) Mr. Carré's bedroom with windows on the south side.
(Bottom) At the back of the bathroom is a sauna. On the left is
a doorway, leading outside.

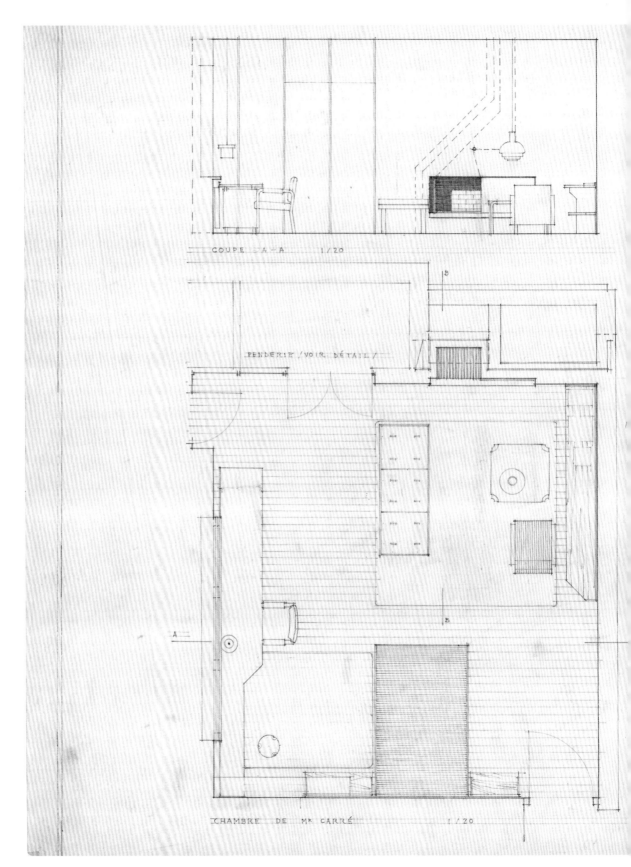

COUPE A-A 1/20

PENDERIE (VOIR DÉTAIL)

CHAMBRE DE Mr CARRÉ 1/20

カレ氏のベッドルームの内装用図面。照明器具の位置や高さ、タンスのディテールまで精確に決めこんでいる

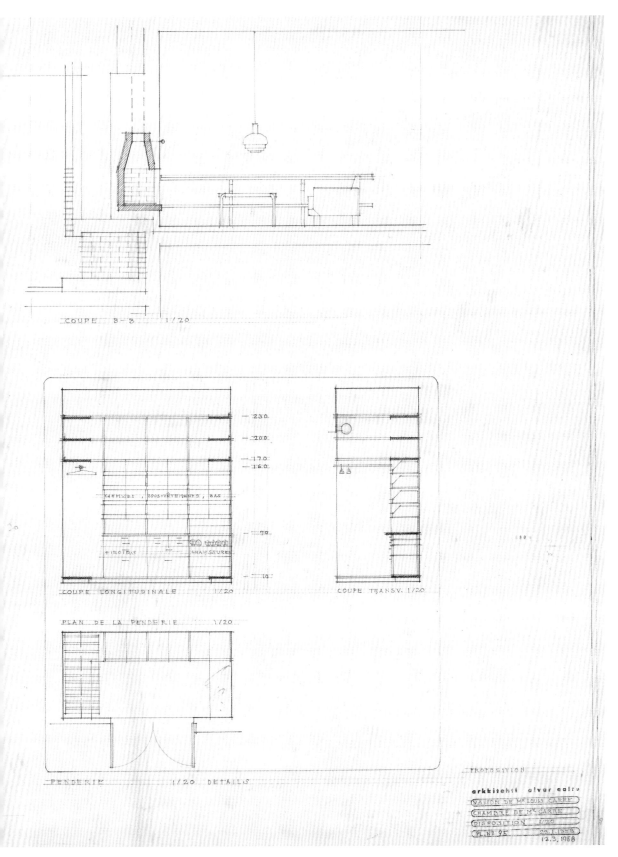

COUPE B-B 1/20

COUPE LONGITUDINALE 1/20

— 230
— 200
— 170
— 160

CHEMISES , SOUS-VÊTEMENTS , BAS

— 70

TIROIRS   CHAUSSURES

— 10

COUPE TRANSV. 1/20

AA

PLAN DE LA PENDERIE 1/20

PENDERIE 1/20 DETAILS

PROPOSITION

arkkitehti alvar aalto

MAISON DE Mr. LOUIS CARRÉ
CHAMBRE DE Mr. CARRÉ
DISPOSITION 1/20
PL. No 95   28.1.1958
                12.3.1958

Interior design drawings for Mr. Carré's bedroom. The location and height of the lighting fixtures and even the details of the closet are drawn with minute precision.

カレ夫人のベッドルーム。部屋の奥にバスルームがつづき、ここにも屋外へ通じる扉がつく

Mrs. Carré's bedroom. The bathroom extends from the back of the room, and has a door opening outside.

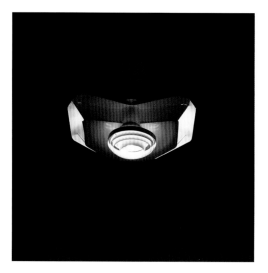

メゾン・カレはアートディーラーの家であり、ライティングは重要な要素である。リビングルームには丸い「ビルベリー(こけもも)ランプ」やサヴォイ・レストラン(1937年)で使われた「ゴールデンベルランプ」が吊りさがる。また、アールトの住宅を訪れると必ず置かれている三連シェードのフロアランプと、素材違いでつくったそのヴァリエーションが見られる。絵を照らすためのダイニングの照明、玄関ホールの波状の天井から吊りさがる直線的な三連のメタルランプなど、ここではアールトの照明デザインが堪能できる

The Maison Carré is the home of an art dealer where lighting is extremely important. The living room has the round Bilberry lamps and the Golden Bell lamps used in the Savoy restaurant (1937). We also find the three-shade-type Angel Wing floor lamp and its variant with different materials. With the dining room lights designed to illuminate paintings on the walls and the metal lamp fixture composed of three sleeve-like parts suspended from the ceiling in the entrance hall, here Aalto's proficiency in illumination design is showcased at its best.

Maison Carré

S 1:600

The client for this house was Louis Carré, an influential Paris art dealer who handled the work of pioneers of modern art including Picasso, Matisse, Léger, and Calder. Aalto had known Léger and Calder since his youth and they were lifelong friends, so it is believed that Carré's commission to Aalto came after the introduction from these common friends. In 1955, Carré wrote a letter to Aalto saying, "I want to build a villa." The location is the small village of Bazoches-sur-Guyonne, about 40 kilometers southwest of Paris. Atop a hill, with its approach threading through a forest of oak, the site looks out over a beautiful pastoral landscape.

From a small gate on the west side, the curving approach climbs gently, the white walls and slanting roof appearing gradually through the trees. It is said that Carré was the one who first asked that the roof be sloping rather than flat, and Aalto's response to the environment of the site is skillful. With the clarity of a single sharp diagonal slicing through the sky against the landscape of the hilltop—its scale matched to the surrounding landscape—the white shape of the house exudes a sense of elegance. We can get a glimpse of the process through which Aalto developed the idea for this house by looking at his early sketches, and what is intriguing is how concerned he was from the outset with how the roofline would be seen.

The sketches show numerous renderings of the shape of the roof in both elevation and section, showing that he closely studied its shape and how it would appear. Alternately taking a bird's-eye view and then a worm's-eye view, he is trying to visualize the lines of the roof and how its volume will emerge both when seen from above and when looked down on from an angle above, or looked up at from below. While the roofline is a very simple slanting line when viewed from the entry-way side, from above, its outline is quite complex, with protrusions and indentations. Evoking the image of Monet's painting of water lilies, the roof spreads out like a flotilla of water lily pads sunk within the forest. The protrusions correspond, on the south side, to the bathrooms of the two bedrooms for Mr. and Mrs. Carré and the small terrace-like spaces extending outside the house from the bathrooms. These two terraces may have been envisioned as out-of-doors places for resting and taking in the sun after a sauna or bath, but they are curious spaces, the necessity of which we remain somehow unconvinced. It is possible that Aalto created these spaces in order to realize his ideas about the shape of the roof.

リビングルームからの眺め。1960 年頃
Panoramic view from the living room in 1960.

この住宅を依頼したルイ・カレは、ピカソ、マティス、レジェ、カルダーなどの作品を扱うパリの有力な画商だった。アールトはレジェやカルダーとは若い頃に知りあい、生涯の友だったが、カレがアールトに住宅を依頼することになったのも、共通のアーティストの友人を介してだったという。場所はパリから車で約1時間、40kmほど南西へ行ったバゾッシュ・シュル・ギュヨンヌ村である。そこはナラの林を縫って登りつめた丘の上、美しい田園風景が眼下に広がる敷地だった。

西側の小さなゲートからゆるやかに湾曲したアプローチを登っていくと、白い壁、片流れの屋根が姿を現してくる。陸屋根ではなく勾配のついた屋根を最初に望んだのはカレの方だったとはいうが、ここでアールトが示した敷地環境への答えは鮮やかである。茫漠とした風景のなか、1本のシャープな斜線で空を切る明快な意識と、ランドスケープに呼応した大きな屋根の存在感。その白い姿は気品すら感じさせる。初期のスケッチを見ると、アールトがこの住宅の発想を膨らませていった形成過程がうかがえるが、興味深いのは最初の段階から屋根の見え方にこだわっている点である。

スケッチでは、屋根のエレベーションやセクション、屋根伏が繰り返し描かれ、形や見え方がスタディされている。アールトの視点は鳥の目になったりカエルの目になったりして、真上から見下ろしたとき、斜め上から見下ろしたとき、下の方から見あげたとき、それぞれ屋根の見え方や量感がどうなるかを視覚化している。玄関側から見るとシンプルな片流れ屋根のラインは、上方からは出っ張ったり引っこんだり、かなり入り組んだ面を考えている。それはまるでモネの描いた「睡蓮」を彷彿とさせ、池に浮かび増殖する睡蓮の葉を拡大して、森のなかに沈めたようなイメージである。出っ張り部分は、南側ではカレ夫妻の各ベッドルームについたバスルームと、そこに隣接して延びる屋外の小さなテラスにあたる。この二つのテラスは、サウナや入浴のあとに外に出て日光浴するのを想定していたのかもしれないが、今一つ必然性に説得力を感じない不思議な空間である。もしかしたらアールトは屋根の形を優先させるために、この空間をつくったのかもしれない。

この住宅で傑出しているのは、外では屋根、内部では天井である。玄関扉を開けると、そこは内側から膨らむような感覚のある大きなヴォリュームのホールである。アカマツの板を張った波打つ天井は、いちばん高いところで5mほどあり、扉の上の大きなハイサイドライトからはドラマチックな光がホールを満たしている。ここは劇場でいう「ホワイエ」にあたり、人が交わるための空間である。アールトはフィンランドからわざわざ大工を呼んで、この天井をつくらせている。ホールはリビングルームと同じくらいの広さを取ってあり、家のなかの動線、たとえば、リビングからダイニングへ、あるいは、リビングから寝室へと移動するときに必ずここを通過するようになっている。

二つのテラスがついた南側ファサード
South facade with two small terraces.

The design of this house excels on the outside in its roof and on the inside with its ceiling. One step inside the entrance, the space opens up in a large hall that feels as if it is swelling out from within. The ceiling is undulating, rising to five meters at its highest, and light floods dramatically into the hall through the large high sidelight over the doorway. This foyer is the grandest part of the house, a place for people to mingle. Aalto brought carpenters from Finland expressly to build this ceiling. The entrance hall occupies about the same amount of space as the living room and lies in the path of movement from one part of the house to another, such as from the living room to dining room, from living room to bedrooms or kitchen.

Maison Carré, being the home of an art dealer, resembles in the attention given to merging art with living space, a concept explored in the Villa Mairea 20 years earlier. They share a number of common techniques. One quality of both houses is the arrangement of space that allows one, while lingering in the entry way, to see all the way into the living room beyond. Moving from the hall into the living room in the Villa Mairea involves going up a flight of four steps, while in the Maison Carré it takes one down a flight of seven steps. In both houses, the steps create a rhythm of physical sensations as one moves smoothly from one space to another. The two houses also share the technique, upon entering from outside, of creating a contrast between the lofty ceiling and the human scale of the walls. In the Villa Mairea, the walls are thick and curving, while in the Maison Carré, two thick white walls parallel one another where paintings can be hung.

The ceiling in the living room in both houses, likewise finished with red-pine slats, not only endows the atmosphere of the room with a special warmth but seems to make the room as a whole into a kind of highly finished furnishing by Aalto. In the Villa Mairea, wood-slatted ceilings are used as effective design elements for uniting and transitioning space. The ceilings in the Maison Carré go even further with extremely fine handling of ceiling height and finishing along the edges.

The Maison Carré follows the spatial techniques used in the Villa Mairea, but if one were to try to capture the distinction between the two houses in a word, it would be that the latter is experimental, while the former is more mature.

玄関ホールからリビングルームを見る
View from the entrance hall toward the living room.

メゾン・カレは画商の家であり、アートを生活空間に融合するのを主眼とする点で、ちょうど20年前に設計されたヴィラ・マイレアとコンセプトを同じくしており、そこでの手法がふんだんに用いられている。たとえば、どちらの家も玄関ホールにたたずむと、視線は長く引っ張られるようにして、その先のリビングルームが垣間見えるようになっている。ホールからリビングへの移動は、ヴィラ・マイレアでは4段の階段を上り、メゾン・カレでは7段下がるかたちで、滑らかなシークエンスのなかにも身体感覚のめりはりをつくっている。また、外からなかへ入ったところで、高い天井とヒューマンスケールの壁を対比させる手法も共通している。ヴィラ・マイレアでは湾曲した厚い白壁、メゾン・カレでは、絵を掛けるための平行に据えた2枚の白壁である。

リビングエリアの天井の仕上げも同じで、細い板張り天井は室内の雰囲気に独特の温かみを添え、部屋全体がアールトの家具のような感じがあり、高い精度を達成している。ヴィラ・マイレアでは、板張り天井は空間をまとめたり、変換したりするための効果的なデザイン要素だった。メゾン・カレの天井はさらにその発展形で、高低差のつけ方、縁の処理のディテールはじつに巧みである。

ヴィラ・マイレアの空間手法に準じたメゾン・カレではあるが、この二つの住宅の明らかな違いを一言でいうならば、前者は「実験的」であり、後者は「成熟」であろう。

当時、遠くまで眺望の開けた西側の斜面は、今では樹木が大きく育って林となり、見晴らしは遮られてしまった。スケッチや図面には植栽が細かく描きこまれたものが多く、アールトは方位に対して空間のヴォリュームを分け、それぞれの窓に違った風景の見え方や光を求めており、建物とランドスケープの構想を同時に練りあげている。見晴らしのよいリビングエリア側（西）のファサードは、シャープな印象の玄関側（北）のファサードとは対照的に、スレート屋根は敷地の傾斜に合わせて下げ、環境に建物を融けこませている。その周囲や前面には土を盛りあげたり低木を植えたりして、自然の林に対して、人が手を入れた植栽を調和させ、さらにはリビングルームから見える景色に遠近感をつくりだしている。一方、ベッドルーム側（南）では、セイナッツァロの役場のように斜面をひな壇状にし、斜面から見あげたときはややモニュメンタルな表情を見せる。

1959年の竣工パーティには、ブラック、カルダー、コクトー、ル・コルビュジエ、シャルロット・ペリアン、アルプ、ジャコメッティ、ギーディオン、マイレ・グリクセンなど、華やかな顔ぶれで359人が出席したという。[1] 1950年代からアールトの仕事の比率は「官」のプロジェクトが多くを占めるようになるが、若い頃から築いてきた芸術家サークルの人脈から実ったこの個人住宅もまた、この建築家の人生の輝かしい1ページを飾るものだったはずだ。

レジェの絵が掛かったリビングルーム
Living room with Léger paintings.

The west side of the Maison Carré once afforded a panorama extending far into the distance, but in the years since the forest has grown up, completely blocking the view. Aalto's sketches and drawings often include details about the trees and shrubs, suggesting how he divided spatial volumes with regard to the directions and orientation of the site and sought to give windows different views and different qualities of light. He thus considered the building simultaneously with landscaping concepts. In contrast to the striking lines of the entrance side (north), the slate roof of the living room facade (west), formerly with a view, slopes at the same angle as the site, making the building seem to merge with its environment. Around and in front of the house earth was mounded up and low trees and plants planted to create a harmony of artificial garden vis-à-vis the native landscape of the site as well as to accentuate the sense of distance in the view from the living room. On the bedroom side (south), meanwhile, the slope is made into tiers, similar to the handling of the slope outside the Säynätsalso Town Hall, so that when seen from below, in the slope, the building assumes a slightly monumental expression.

The story goes that the completion party was a gala affair attended by 359 guests including such names as Braque, Calder, Cocteau, Le Corbusier, Charlotte Perriand, Arp, Giacometti, Giedion, and Maire Gullichsen.[1] From the 1950s, Aalto's fame spread from his work on major public projects, but private home designs like this one, done for clients through artistic celebrities, were likewise highlights of his career as an architect.

低木を植えこんだ西側
West facade surrounded with shrubs.

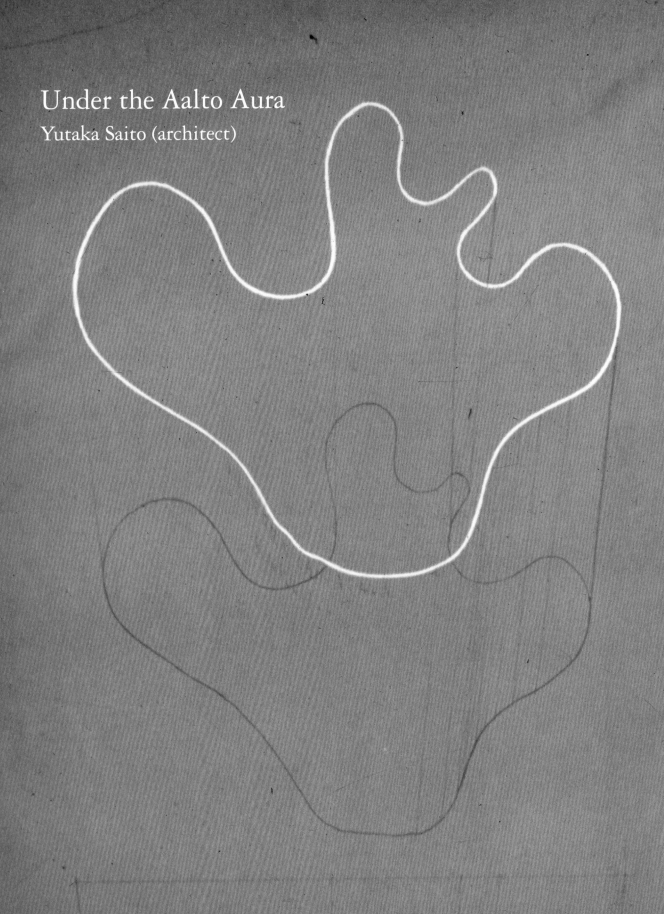

Under the Aalto Aura
Yutaka Saito (architect)

Some architects create works that reveal the traces of the primal landscapes and formative experiences of their lives. Frank Lloyd Wright, Luis Barragán, Antonio Gaudi, and Carlo Scarpa are typical examples. Alvar Aalto was among them. He may have been influenced by Modern Art artists like Jean Arp and Constantin Brancusi in the gentle curves and free forms he used in designs from large buildings to lamps, but the images evoked in them—the varied shapes of lakes, the shifting colors of water, islands in the waters of lakes, stands of red pine and birch, dazzling colors of autumn, snow, the iced-over seas, the white arctic night—are of the landscape of Finland. Even while he was designing the Paimio Tuberculosis Sanatorium, the Viipuri City Library, and other works under the influence of functionalism in the late 1920s and early 1930s, Aalto was pursuing somewhere in his work a resonance with the land. His houses built in planned residential lots, too, consistently sought approaches connecting the building to the special character of the site.

Finger Forms

In studying the sketches and drawings of many of Aalto's works, his house designs included, one notices the recurrent motif of shapes like an open palm, or baseball mitt, in the abstract resembling a fan. The motif seems to display not so much just an open palm as a fist that now and then opens, closes, and sticks out fingers as in a game of rock-stone-scissors. "Finger form" might describe it better than "hand form." Aalto's attachment to this motif was so strong that it appears to have arisen from something like the realm of the subconscious. For Aalto, the finger form was a point of departure for the imagination, a pattern from which infinite applications could be spun.

As a boy, Aalto is said to have aspired to become an artist, and he was an architect who loved drawing pictures and forms. The finger form, however, displays something more primordial than the result of an artist's sketching. Central Finland, the land where Aalto

アールトの大きな傘の下で

齋藤 裕 （建築家）

フィンガーフォーム ———————————————————

　建築家には、その人物の原風景や原体験が透けて見えるような作品をつくる人がいる。フランク・ロイド・ライト、ルイス・バラガン、アントニオ・ガウディ、カルロ・スカルパなどはその典型である。アルヴァ・アールトもそんな一人だ。大きな建築から照明にいたるまで、柔らかな曲線、フリーフォームを使ったのは、アルプやブランクーシといったモダンアート作品の影響があったにしても、そこから喚起されるイメージはフィンランドの風土である。湖の変化に富んだ形、刻々と移り変わる水の色、水上に浮かぶ小島、垂直に伸びたアカマツやシラカバの森、目の覚めるような紅葉、雪、氷海、白夜の光……。パイミオのサナトリウム、ヴィープリの図書館などを建設し、機能主義（ファンクショナリズム）の影響下にあった 1920 年代後半から 30年代前半の頃でさえも、アールトは作品のどこかに風土と共振するものを求めている。区画された住宅地に建てるときでさえ、敷地と建物とを関連づけ、そこから答えを探しだす取りくみは一貫して変わらない姿勢だった。

　住宅に限らず、アールトのスケッチやプランを通して見ていると、繰り返し現れてくる形があるのに気づく。指を広げた手形のような、ともいえるし、野球のグローブのような、ともいえる。抽象的な目で見れば、扇形ともいえる。それがじゃんけんの「グー・チョキ・パー」のような、拳を握りしめたり、指を出したりするパターンをつくっているので、手形というよりフィンガーフォームといった方が近いかもしれない。この形へのこだわりようは、無意識の域に近いところから出てきているのではないかと思わせるほど強い。アールトにとって、イマジネーションを鼓舞する出発点となる形、無限の応用力を秘めた形がこのフィンガーフォームだったのだ。

　アールトは少年時代、画家になりたいと思っていたという。たしかに彼は絵心がある建築家だ。けれども、この形には絵筆をもって描く以前の、もっと原初的な印象がある。彼が育ったフィ

was reared, is buried in snow for more than half the year. Any child who has grown up in this snow country has played by making handprints on frost- or mist-covered windowpanes or footprints in white blankets of new snow. The resulting shapes always change, as when water droplets form and run down a windowpane or when footprints erode or melt away. For children, those changing forms are endlessly fascinating. They delight in the unexpected shapes they can create with overlapping handprints, pressed on at slightly different angles and with different rhythms. It is up to the child to think how much space to allow so that the form stands out in its frame. They also learn the interesting effects that can be achieved by throwing off the symmetry or giving the shapes a twist or deformation. Children know how such little discoveries about form can be applied in ever-larger ways.

Aalto went on exploring his fascination with finger forms throughout his life. He extended his applications of these forms freely, to vases, furnishings, buildings, and even to plans for communities and cities. From his boyhood he seems to have unconsciously cultivated this sense for the infinite varieties and rhythms of form and space. After becoming an architect, he manipulated them in different ways, aligning different shapes along a straight line, combining straight lines and curved lines, and creating rhythms by combining not only two but three forms of similar shape. This trend in his work seems to have surfaced in notable form around the 1950s, and after that it recurs, in new and distinct variations, repeated and applied over and over.

Many of Aalto's sketches, made as he endeavored to grasp the scale of a building, have been preserved, but what is startling about these small drawings often found in the margins is that, if one enlarges them one finds that they are all in exact proportion to the actual size of the building. In this capacity so indispensable to architects and sculptors, Aalto had extraordinary talent; he was able to freely envision an image in his head, enlarge or reduce it accurately, and three-dimensionalize it.

イタリア・パヴィア近郊の都市計画。1966 年
Suburban planning project near Pavia, Italy. 1966.

ンランド中部は、一年の半分近くは雪が降る。そんな雪国の子供がきまってするのは、結露した窓に手を置いて手形をつけたり、真っ白な新雪に足跡をつけたりする遊びだ。その形は、水滴が流れて滲んできたり、崩れてきたり、溶けたり、つねに変化していく。子供にはその変化がたまらなく面白い。あるいは、手形をたくさん、角度をずらしながら重ねていく。すると、思いもよらない形に変容したり、リズムが出てきたりして楽しげに見える。どのくらい余白を取れば絵の存在感が引きたつかも、その子の勘所だ。シンメトリーをはずし、形にずれやゆがみを加えることで、絵はもっと面白くなる。子供はそんな単純で小さな発見がどんどん大きく膨らんでいくのをよく知っている。

　アールトは、このフィンガーフォーム遊びを一生つづけた建築家だと思う。それを花瓶から家具、建築、都市計画まで、自在に広げていった。形の無限の広がりや余白の感覚、リズム感は、幼少時代から知らず知らずのうちに培われていったのだろう。建築家になってからは、形をまとめるために軸になる1本の線を加えたり、直線と曲線とを組みあわせたり、同じ形を二つではなく三つに組んでリズムをつくったりする操作を加えていく。それはいつからなのか。フィンガーフォームが顕著になるのは、1950年代頃からだ。その後、変奏曲のようにつぎつぎとヴァリエーションを広げ、操作し、駆使していく。

　ところで、建物のスケール感をつかもうとして、フリーハンドで描かれたアールトのスケッチが数多く残されているが、それを見ると、紙の端に小さく描かれた絵でも、数倍に拡大してみるとプロポーションが実際の建築と違っていないのには驚く。頭にあるイメージを自由に、しかも正確に縮小したり拡大したりして描写し、立体化する術、これは建築家や彫刻家に必要不可欠な能力だが、彼はこれに関しては飛び抜けている。

　アールトにとって、フィンガーフォームがどれほど設計の源泉となっていたかは、小さな住宅から大きな建築まで、プランを時系列で俯瞰してみれば明らかである（主要作品プラン参照）。それにしても、アールトの才能とは、これを生涯つづけたことではなかろうか。誰しも子供のときに脳裏に刻みついた風景や形の記憶はあるにちがいないが、それを飽きずに、一生を通して創作の原点にしつづけるのはむずかしい。とくに大人になればなるほど、それがばからしく

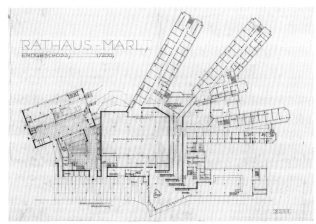

ドイツ・マール市・行政機関のコンペ案。1957年
Competition proposal for town hall and administrative offices in Marl, Germany. 1957.

We can see how consistently the finger form motif formed the prototype of Aalto's designs by organizing his works, from small houses to large buildings, along a time line (see Plans of Major Works). One wonders if his genius actually lay in continuing to apply this motif throughout his whole career. Everyone must have memories of scenes and forms that are deeply imprinted on their memory in childhood, but it is not often that such patterns continue to be the basis of a person's creative work throughout life. Particularly when a person reaches adulthood, such forms or scenes usually begin to appear nonsensical; the more knowledge we acquire, the less such images influence us. Perhaps Aalto continued to draw on finger forms as the source of his creative inspiration for such a long time because he was an architect who never quite outgrew his youth. Some may chide me, declaring that the concepts of great architects and artists are not so simplistic. But I have found that in many cases, the spark that fuels creativity arises from surprisingly simple motifs that could easily be dismissed as childish. We can see why so many of Aalto's lifelong friends were artists: Fernand Léger, László Moholy-Nagy, and Alexander Calder. And yet, a childlike innocence is one of the noblest attributes of an artist. The relationship between these people and Aalto was a bond transcending words; it was based on an intuitive empathy for each other.

Influence of Asplund

Before his meeting with the pioneers of the Modern Art movement, Aalto had been greatly influenced by the work of Swedish architect Erik Gunnar Asplund. In the 1920s, he frequently visited Asplund's works and was inspired by them.

The essence of Asplund's architecture is use of the formal proportions of simple geometry. His works have an aura that measures and commands the environment in which they stand. All architecture students are required to study classical proportions in classes

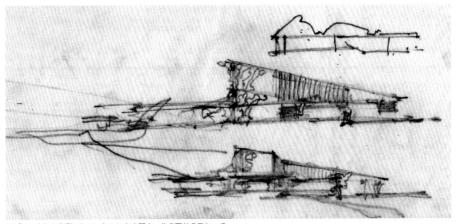

メゾン・カレの北側エレベーションと玄関ホールの天井のスケッチ
North elevation and the entrance-hall-ceiling sketches for Maison Carré.

思えてきたりする。知識をつけていけばいくほど、その影は薄くなっていく。アールトが万年少年の心をもちつづけた建築家だったからこそ、ひたすらフィンガーフォームを創作の源泉にできたのではないか。巨匠といわれる建築家やアーティストの着想はそんな単純なものではない、と笑われるかもしれない。だが意外にも、創作意欲の火を煽るのは、拍子抜けするほど単純で、はたから見れば子供っぽいと思われかねないモティーフが原動力になっている場合も多い。アールトにアーティストの友人が多かったのもうなずける。レジェやモホリ・ナジをはじめ、カルダーとは生涯の友だった。童心こそアーティストの最大の資質である。アールトと彼らとの関係は、言葉を超えて、たがいに直感的に感応する結びつきがあったのだろう。

アスプルンドからの影響 ──────────────

　モダンアートを牽引していったアーティストたちと出会う前、アールトに多大な影響を及ぼしたのがスエーデンの建築家エリック・グンナール・アスプルンドだった。1920 年代、アールトは足繁くアスプルンドの作品を見てまわり、感化を受ける。

　アスプルンドの建築の心髄は、単純幾何学を使ったフォーマルなプロポーションの駆使にある。その作品は周囲の環境を律し、支配するほどのオーラを放つ。建築史の授業で古典のプロポーションを学ぶのは建築学科の学生の必修だが、幾何学を建築に応用する術は今も昔も大学では教わらない。社会に出てから、その術を自家薬籠中の物にできるかどうかは個人の資質だ。アスプルンドの建築手法は、複数の正方形や正三角形を重ね、$1:2$、$1:3$、$1:\sqrt{2}$、$1:\sqrt{3}$ といった素数比例を組みあわせて形をつくり、それを連続させてまとめるものだ。さらに、そこで使われるディテールは凝りすぎず、だが細心の注意がすみずみまで行きとどいており、建築の完成度が高められている。

　アールトはこの世界に憧れた。まだ大学出立ての頃、アスプルンドの事務所に就職しようとするが断られてしまう。このあたりの経緯はヨーラン・シルツの伝記[2]に詳しいが、のちに新進気鋭の建築家としてアールトが頭角を現してくると、アスプルンドはその才能を大いに認める。アールトより13 歳年上のこの建築家が亡くなる1940 年まで、二人の間では温かな交流が途切れ

アスプルンド設計、森の墓地・礼拝堂
Woodland Cemetery and Chapel by Erik Gunnar Asplund.

on architectural history, but universities did not in the past and do not today teach them how to apply geometry in architecture. Whether or not an architect can acquire that ability after launching upon a career is up to the individual. Asplund's architectural method consisted of combining multiple squares and equilateral triangles in shapes combined in proportions of prime numbers 1:2, 1:3, 1:$\sqrt{2}$, 1:$\sqrt{3}$, and completing the form by the repetition of these forms. He perfected his works by simplifications and refinements made through the utmost attention to the smallest detail.

Aalto yearned to be part of this architectural world. Soon after graduating from university, he applied for a job at Asplund's firm but was rejected, an experience that is described in detail by Göran Schildt.[2] Later, when Aalto began to establish his reputation as an upcoming member of the architectural avant garde, Asplund was among those who generously recognized his talent, and from then until Asplund, 13 years Aalto's senior, passed away in 1940, they maintained a constant and cordial relationship.

But Aalto, unsuccessful in becoming a formal student of the mentor he worshiped at the outset of his career, was forced to forge his own path. Taking advantage of his links with functionalism and the pioneers of the Modern Art movement, he explored his own forms of expression and expanded the scope of his work. The methodology he gradually established from this time actually moved in a direction opposite to the work of Asplund, deliberately avoiding symmetry and squares and skewing the geometry of simple forms. Stimulated by Modern Art, such as by cubist works created by the recombination of dismantled elements, he broke away from the proportions of formal architecture and added spontaneous elements through the insertion of curves and diagonals.

Unlike painting or sculpture, of course, architecture depends upon the rational and economical combination of materials, and cannot be built with free forms alone. Geometry is indispensable. With what he learned from Asplund as his base, Aalto sought to create his

ヴィラ・マイレアの窓プロポーション
Window proportions. Villa Mairea.

ることはなかった。

　だが、建築をはじめる第一歩で、崇拝するアスプルンドに正式な弟子として受けいれてもらえなかったアールトは、自分の進むべき道を探さなければならなかった。このとき、彼は機能主義の潮流や第一線のモダンアートの担い手たちとの結びつきをきっかけに自分の表現を探り、枠を押し広げようとする。この頃から徐々に確立していったのが、むしろアスプルンドとは正反対の世界で、シンメトリーや正方形を避け、幾何学的な単純形態にひずみを加えていく方法だった。モダンアートからの刺激、たとえば、解体した要素を重ねあわせて再構成するキュビストの作品のように、フォーマルな建築のプロポーションを崩し、曲線や斜線を加えたりして即興的な要素を加えていく。もちろん建築は絵画や彫刻と違って、合理的・経済的に素材を組みあわせて構成していかねば成り立たないものだから、フリーフォームだけではつくれない。幾何学は絶対に不可欠だ。アールトは、アスプルンドから学んだことを下敷きに、たとえば正方形を避けた 8:9 や 1:$\sqrt{5}$ といった、ほかの建築家が使わないプロポーションで独自の建築の世界を築こうとした。その発展形に、フィンガーフォームがある。

中庭への愛着

　つぎに、アールトの取りくみで特徴的なのが、「土地の読み」である。彼は土地の形状を最大限に活かそうと、敷地に少しでも高低差があればそれを取りこんで設計し、特徴を与えようとしてきた。住宅においても、たとえばロヴァニエミにあるメゾン・アホのように、区画整理された平凡な住宅地に建てる場合であっても、下り傾斜の敷地に対してプランを台形にし、内部の見え方にパースペクティブをつくって土地の長さを強調した。

　もう一つの特徴が、閉じる構成である。環境に対して建築の形をいったん壁で閉じる。そこに中庭を取る。そして、閉じた上で一部あるいは半分を開く手法だ。厳寒の国だから、閉じるのが基本になるのは当たり前だという人もいるかもしれないが、彼がそうしたのは気候のためではない。たとえば、ムーラッツァロ島にあるアールトの夏の家。湖に向けて 180 度視界の広がる風光明媚な敷地にあって、アールトはほぼ四方を閉じている。なぜこの場所でここまで閉じ

アールト夏の家
Aalto Summer House.

own designs in proportions not used by other architects, of 8:9 or $1{:}\sqrt{5}$, avoiding regular squares, for example. The finger forms were his ways of developing those shapes.

Courtship of the Courtyard

Aalto's architecture stands out, too, for his skill in "reading" the site and incorporating its features into his designs, taking advantage of even the smallest differences in elevation. For private homes even, building on an ordinary zoned plot of land such as for the Maison Aho in Rovaniemi, he planned the house in a trapezoidal shape following the downward slope of the property, creating a sense of interior perspective that emphasizes the length of the house.

Composition of enclosure is another noteworthy feature of his architecture. First, a wall demarcates the shape of the building vis-à-vis its surroundings, and a courtyard is created. Then, working from that closure, part or half is then opened up. In a country of intense cold, one might assume closure to be an obvious governing principle of space, and yet his reference point is not just the climate. Take, for example, Aalto's Summer House on Muuratsalo island. Situated facing the scenic waters of the lake, Aalto nevertheless closed the house on all four sides. Why should a house built on a splendid scenic vantage point be closed? Even after visiting the house several times, I was only able to answer this question after having stayed there overnight. It is difficult to completely grasp the importance to this house of the centripetal power of the red-brick-wall-surrounded courtyard without spending a certain amount of time there. To enjoy the scenery outside, one need only step outside the wall. Aalto's attention, however, was focused on the time that would be spent there with friends or family. The interior is extremely simple. But one is struck by the courtyard's presence when it is an arena of dining and conversation, and also by our sense of the architect's devotion to the space and its richness.

夏の家のスケッチ
Sketch for Aalto Summer House.

なければならないのか。何度か訪れてその疑問への答えが実感できたのは、ここに泊まったときだった。赤レンガで囲んだ中庭の求心力の強さ──それがこの住宅にどれほど大事な要素かは、ある程度長い時間を過ごしてみないと実感できない。外の景色を楽しみたいなら塀を一歩出ればすむことだ。それよりもアールトの意図は、ここで友人たちと過ごす時間に向けられている。内部のつくりはいたって簡素だ。だが、みなが集まって食事をし、団欒の場である中庭の存在感、そこに込められた思い、空間の密度は濃い。

　建築家が自分のために建てた家を見ると、その作家の体質や性格が全体の雰囲気に滲みでているように感じられるが、アールトという人は、人懐こくて生来の淋しがり屋だったのかもしれない。たとえば、ルイス・バラガンの自邸のテーマは「孤独」だ。彼は孤独に浸るのを好み、それを楽しむ空間を進んで求めた建築家だった。一方アールトは、誰かと一緒にいる空間を想定する人であり、空間単位はつねに二人以上である。

　伝記作家のヨーラン・シルツは、アールトは若い頃から北イタリアの建築に強い憧れを抱き、それを生涯インスピレーションの源泉にしたと書いている。1924年、新婚旅行でアールトは初めてイタリアを訪れているが、のちに、「私の心のなかにはいつもイタリアへの旅がある」[3]と語っている。勢力争いが繰り返されたイタリア都市国家の歴史のなかで、表に対しては壁で閉じて防御を固めつつ、そのなかに中庭や光庭、広場をつくり、内部で繰り広げられる生活の質を高め、洗練させてきたイタリアの建築文化、それを知れば知るほど惹かれるのは、建築家ならば当然であろう。アールトのイタリアへの中庭の執着が強く感じられるのが、セイナッツァロの役場の中庭だ。ヨーラン・シルツはこの作品について、「アールトは建物で囲んだこの中庭を、シエナのカンポ広場のように全市民が集う場所と想定していた。今のところそのようには使われていないが、おそらく彼は、セイナッツァロでの地域生活を理想化して頭に描いたのだろう」[4]と指摘している。

　あるいは、「閉じたなかの中庭」という発想は、フィンランドの古民家にも見られる。よく引きあいに出されるのが、ヘルシンキのセウラサーリ野外博物館に保存されている「ニエメラ」という民家だ。これは中部地方の農家で、母屋、サウナ、家畜小屋、穀物倉などが円を描くよ

セイナッツァロの役場の中庭
Courtyard of Säynätsalo Town Hall.

Observing a house that an architect builds for himself, one feels as if it exudes the atmosphere of its author's character and personality. Aalto seems to have been extremely sociable, yearning for constant companionship. By contrast, the theme of Luis Barragán's own house is solitude. Barragán enjoyed steeping himself in solitude and was an architect who actively created spaces for savoring the awarness of being apart. The basic premise of Aalto's space, however, was that of companionship; his spaces are consistently meant for two or more people.

Göran Schildt writes that Aalto as a young man was much attracted to the architecture of northern Italy and drew inspiration from it throughout his career. He first visited there on his honeymoon in 1924, but is later said to have remarked that, "In my mind, there is always a journey to Italy."[3] The architectural culture of Italy, shaped by a history of recurrent struggles among powerful rival families, evolved within walls closed tightly in defense against the outside. Inside those walls, people built courtyards, light courts, and piazzas within which they developed and refined the quality of their daily lives. It is not surprising that architects become fascinated with this architecture the more they learn about it. Aalto's attraction to the Italian courtyard may be felt strongly in the courtyard of the Säynätsalo Town Hall. Schildt writes regarding this work: "Aalto envisaged the raised courtyard enclosed by the various buildings as a place for all citizens to assemble in the manner of Siena's Campo. This has not happened so far, perhaps because Aalto idealized community life in Säynätsalo . . ."[4]

The idea of the courtyard within enclosure can also be seen in the folk houses of Finland, as exemplified by the often-cited Niemelä house at the Seurasaari Open Air Museum in Helsinki. A dwelling from the central region of the country, it consists of a main house, sauna, stable, and granary built around a central courtyard. The smoke sauna dates from the early 1700s and the main house from around 1840. The principle of individual

フィンランドの古民家「ニエメラ」。18世紀から19世紀にかけての建造物
Niemelä, Finnish traditional house built between the 18th and 19th centuries.

うに建てられ、中央は中庭になっている。スモークサウナは1700年代、母屋は1840年頃の建物という。機能別に建物を分けて建て、全体を中庭がまとめているのだが、これはまさにアールトの十八番の手法だ。表通りに対しては閉じるが、裏には庭や中庭に向かって開く形になる。住宅を依頼された作曲家ヨーナス・コッコネンとの会話で、アールトはこのように述べている。「個人住宅は、通りに対してどのように配置しなければならないかわかりますか？　通り側へは背中を向け、中庭側へ家の顔を向けるべきなのです」[5]

北国の光 —————————————————————

　フィンランドでは、12月下旬の冬至前後から2月初旬にかけては、朝9時頃に太陽が昇り、夕方4時頃には沈む。一方、6月下旬から8月まで白夜である。寒い国では明るさ以上に光のぬくもりが求められるはずだから、光量の多い南向きがいちばん尊ばれるかというと、アールトの場合そうではない。この本の10作品のなかで、ヴィラ・タンメカンとヴィラ・オクサラのリビングルームは南向き、メゾン・アホは北向き、ほかの7作品は西向きである。午前中よりも午後からの光を楽しむ家の方が圧倒的に多いのだ。

　とはいえ、主要ベッドルームはきまって東向きで、朝の光が窓から入ってくるように設計されている。一方、リビングルームやダイニングルームは午前中の直射光は入らず、西向きに大きく開かれる。北国は夕日が美しい。私も北海道に建てた家で、太陽が小山の向こうに沈むぎりぎりまで夕日を満喫できるよう、ダイニングルームの窓を西向きに大きくしたことがある。ましてフィンランドでは白夜がある。リビングやダイニングを西向きにすれば、夏には夜の9時頃まで自然光が楽しめるのだ。

　あるいは、ヴィラ・シルツのように、ある特別の風景と光を得るのを焦点に設計された家もある。この家では、リビングルームの窓は南西方向へ折り曲げるようにして張りだしてあるが、冬の晴れた日には、そこから日没が見られる。さらにその方向には、葦の繁った人の手が入っていない入り江の景色を眺められる。どの住宅についても、どちら側へ向けて窓を大きく開くかは、敷地を見たとき、アールトのなかでは瞬時に出てくる答えだっただろう。各部屋での過ご

ヴィラ・マイレアのダイニングルーム
Dining room. Villa Mairea.

エンソ・グッツァイト社宅Bの窓まわり
Window details. Enso-Gutzeit House B.

structures for different functions united into a whole around a central courtyard is exactly Aalto's modus operandi. Although perhaps closed to the street or world outside, his houses are open to their garden or courtyard in back. In conversations with composer Joonas Kokkonen, who had commissioned Aalto to build his home, the architect is said to have stated: "Do you know how a private house must be situated in relation to the road? The road must be at the back and the facade must face the yard."[5]

Northern Light

In Finland from the winter solstice in late December to early February, the sun comes up around 9:00 a.m. and goes down around 4:00 p.m. From late June until August is the season of "white nights." In a cold country where the sun is valued even more for its warmth than its light, one might expect that well-lit southern exposures would be most highly prized, and yet in Aalto's case this is not always so. Of the 10 works introduced in this book, only two—Villa Tammekann and Villa Oksala—have living rooms facing south. Maison Aho faces north and the other seven face west. The majority are designed to enjoy the sun not in the morning but in the afternoon.

Nevertheless, the master bedrooms face east, planned so that the morning sun floods through their windows. The living and dining rooms, meanwhile, admit little direct light during the morning and have windows opening toward the west. After all, sunset in the northlands is beautiful. In a house I built in Hokkaido, I, too, enlarged the west window of the dining room, the better to prolong the view of the sun setting beyond a hill to the west. In Finland, which has white nights in the summertime if the living and dining rooms face west, they enjoy natural lighting until 9:00 p.m. during the summertime.

Some of Aalto's houses, like the Villa Schildt, are deliberately oriented to take advantage of a particular landscape or angle of light. The living room of the Schildt house,

ヴィラ・シルツ
Villa Schildt.

し方にいちばん適切な光の質や量を考えてプランをつくっているのだ。アールトは、風景と光を特別なものにするためによく出窓をつけるが、ローコスト住宅であっても、窓に対する予算は可能な限りかけ、絶対におとさない。

大きな傘の下 ─────────────

アールトの個人住宅には、三つのグループがあるという。[6] まず、友人やその縁で依頼されたもので、クライアントの顔もライフスタイルも、好みも知って設計したもの。つぎに、企業から依頼された、たとえばスンマのエンソ・グッツァイトの社宅や、スニラのマネージャーの家など、そこに誰が住むかはわからないが、社会的地位に相応の暮らしを想定して設計したもの。三つめは、スタンダードハウス。これはとくに戦前から戦後にかけてアールトがプランづくりに心血を注いだもので、戦争で家を失った人々や工場労働者など、低所得者層に向けて設計された。工場生産でプレファブ化し、簡単迅速に建設できるもので、家族構成、敷地環境など、個別の条件にフレキシブルに対応できるように考えられている。

この本では、アールトが出した答えが、敷地環境や住む者への特殊解になっているかを選ぶポイントにした。この場所だからこの答え、この人が住むからこの答えと、アールトが特殊条件の「読み」にどのくらい思考を傾けているか。そんなアプローチが濃厚に感じとれるものを選んでいる。そのため、二つめと三つめのグループは入れていない。

例外はエンソ・グッツァイトの社宅で、これは特定の施主のための設計ではないが、敷地環境との関係が色濃く反映されていることから加えた。また、この社宅は三つめのグループであるスタンダードハウスとも関連してくる。アールトは住環境を整備・向上しようと、何百パターンもの住宅プランを考案し、規格化を目指した。この知的鍛錬の積み重ねが彼の頭のなかに蓄積されていたからこそ、エンソ・グッツァイトのような、こなれたプランによる質の高い社宅がつくられたのだ。

ヴィラ・マイレアの施主の息子で建築家のクリスチャン・グリクセンは、「戦後、アールトはそこ（戦前に築いた独自の表現）へふたたび戻ろうとはしなかった」[7] と語っている。アールト作

ユヴァスキラのアルヴァ・アールト・ミュージアム
Alvar Aalto Musuem in Jyväskylä (1971−74).

for example, projects from the house so that its picture window faces southwest, affording a view of the sunset on clear winter days and a still-wild, reed-filled inlet on the lake. Aalto seems to have instinctively known which way each house he designed should face the moment he saw the site. He clearly drew his plans based on careful consideration of the appropriate quality and volume of light needed, depending on the purpose of the room. He often added bay windows to his designs to capture particular vistas or qualities of light, and even in low-cost housing projects, he tried not to cut costs on windows.

Under the Aalto Aura

Aalto's private homes fall into three groups.[6] One is made up of designs done for friends or requested through friends, for which he knew the clients well and was familiar with their lifestyle and tastes. The second group consists of commissions from corporations, such as for the Enso-Gutzeit houses at Summa and the manager's house at Sunila. In these cases, he did not know who would be living in the houses but created his designs premised on a lifestyle for people of a certain social stratum. The third group was of standard houses. He devoted himself heart and soul to this category of housing especially from the pre-World War II to postwar era, aiming his designs for factory workers and low-income earners who had lost their homes in the war. He devised ways for mass production of prefabricated units to allow for simple, fast construction and developed designs that could be adapted flexibly depending on family composition, characteristics of the site, and other special conditions.

The works chosen for this book are those that feature Aalto's special solutions for particular environments or residents. I have chosen them for the idiosyncrasy of their approaches, examining the extent to which Aalto focused his thinking on his reading of special conditions, coming up with one answer for one sort of environment and another

イマトラ・三つ十字の教会
Three Crosses Church in Imatra (1955−58).

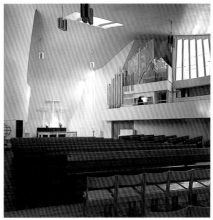

教会内部
Interior space of the church.

品のなかでも抜きんでて完成度の高いヴィラ・マイレアはまた、突出して表現主義的で実験的な作品であり、のちの作品の「胚芽」的なものだった。シルカリーサ・イェッツォネンは、「アールトは必要を美に変容させつつ、小さなディテールからはじめて、テーマを洗練し多様化していった。（中略）その一方、ディテールから家具、一つの作品、大規模な建築群にいたるまで、同じテーマが異なるスケールで繰り返し現れた」[8]と書く。

　たしかに、アールトはディテールや素材、エレメントの形などを縮小したり、拡大したり、用途を変えたりして繰り返し使った。だが同時に、グリクセンがいうように、ヴィラ・マイレアで築いた世界に戦後戻らなかったのもたしかだ。つまり、建築へのアプローチを変えたのだ。それには、戦争という大きな節目を無視することはできないだろう。以降、アールトはヴィラ・マイレアのような、着地点の見えない実験的なアプローチはしなくなる。むしろ、これまで彼が蓄積したものを規格化し、アレンジし、ヴァリエーションを広げ、洗練させる方向へ向かった。この取りくみ方は、とくに住宅で顕著だ。ヴィラ・マイレアの延長線上にメゾン・カレ、セイナッツァロの役場の延長線上にアールトの夏の家、フィンガーフォームとタイプデザインを掛けあわせたエンソ・グッツァイト社宅やヴィラ・シルツ、ヴィラ・コッコネンなど。ただし、各作品の完成度の高さや密度の濃さは、アールト事務所の担当者の腕によって幅があるのも否めない。

　住宅に限らず、商業施設、公共建築などいろいろな作品を見てまわっていると、いつも私の頭に思い浮かぶのが、「アールトの大きな傘の下」という言葉だ。象徴的にいえば「アールトのオーラの下」、実際的にいえば、「ディレクション能力」という意味であり、これはきわめて現代的な建築家の仕事のやり方。ヨーラン・シルツの作成したリスト[9]によると、開設以来、アールト事務所に出入りしたスタッフの数は総勢360人にのぼり、スイス人、デンマーク人、スエーデン人をはじめ、戦後はアメリカ人、イタリア人、日本人、インド人など、国籍もさまざまだ。ヨーロッパ諸国のなかで、独自のアイデンティティをもつのは20世紀に入ってからとなった国フィンランドにあって、ユニヴァーサルでありつつローカリティを強く打ちだし、人々の耳目を磁石のように吸い寄せる建築をつくったアールト。その観点から見れば、彼の方法論は現代の建築家に共通するものであり、また、その先駆者でもあった。

庭からサウナへの眺め。ヴィラ・マイレア
View toward the sauna hut through the garden. Villa Mairea.

answer for such and such a resident. As a result, I have not included works representative of the second and third groups.

The exception is the Enso-Gutzeit company housing, which was not designed for a specific owner-client but is included because it reflects Aalto's close consideration for the environment of the site in his design. This work is also linked to his work with the standard houses of the third group. Seeking to develop and improve housing environments, Aalto devised hundreds of housing plans and sought to standardize them. The high quality of his plan for company-provided management housing such as the Enso-Gutzeit houses was the fruition of the professional acumen he had accumulated in that process.

Architect Kristian Gullichsen, son of the owner of Villa Mairea, has observed that after the war, Aalto "didn't pick up the same language as before."[7] The Villa Mairea, one of the most highly perfected of Aalto's works is also an outstandingly expressionist and experimental work that provided the germ of ideas for later works. Sirkkaliisa Jetsonen notes how, "Starting with small details, he refines and varies different themes, making necessity a virtue . . . On the other hand, the same themes keep recurring at different scales, from details and furniture all the way to buildings and even groups of buildings."[8]

Aalto did indeed reduce and enlarge the shapes of details, materials, and elements, using and reusing them in different applications. Nevertheless, as Gullichsen noted, he did not return to his prewar vocabulary of design. Rather, he changed his approach to architecture. The role of the war as the watershed of that change cannot be ignored. From that time onward, Aalto no longer took off on experimental flights—for which there was no guarantee where they might come to rest—that he had ventured in such works as the Villa Mairea. Rather he turned in the direction of the standardization of designs he had previously accumulated, modifying them and expanding their variation and refinement.

These postwar efforts are particularly notable in his houses—the Maison Carré on the

さまざまな建築エレメントと素材の調和。ヴィラ・マイレア
Harmonious combination of diverse architectural elements and materials. Villa Mairea.

extension of the Villa Mairea, the Aalto Summer House on the extension of the Säynätsalo Town Hall, and the Enso-Gutzeit company houses, Villa Schildt and Villa Kokkonen as combinations of finger form and type design concepts, and so on. There is some undeniable variation in the level of perfection and the intensity of the design depending on who was in charge of the project at Aalto's office.

The image that always comes into my mind when I am touring Aalto's works, not only his houses, but his commercial buildings and public edifices as well, is of being "under the Aalto umbrella"—figuratively speaking the "Aalto aura"—but in practical terms under his "power of direction." For as an architect his approach to work was very much the product of contemporary times. According to Schildt's listing of his works, the number of staff who came and went from Aalto's firm from the time it opened totaled some 360.[9] They included not only Swiss, Danes, and Swedes, but, after World War II, Americans, Italians, Japanese, Indians, among other nationalities. Based in Finland, a country among European nations that had only acquired an identity of its own after the turn of the twentieth century, Aalto boldly asserted a message of universality and locality in architecture that had an almost irresistible appeal. Looked at from this perspective, his methods have much in common with the architects of our era today—in fact, he was their forerunner.

アールト自邸とスタジオ
Aalto House & Studio
Helsinki, Finland (1935 – 1936)

北東側の道路から見た玄関ファサード
Facade from street on northeast side.

南側の窓。正方形をはずしたアールト独特のプロポーション
South window. Here we see distinctively Aalto proportions in the shifted squares.

道路に面しては窓を開けずに壁だけの量感で構成する

On the street side, the facade design features only a massive wall, without any windows.

通り側へは背中を向け、庭側へは家の顔を向けるべきです——アルヴァ・アールト
The road must be at the back and the facade must face the garden. ——Alvar Aalto

庭は一つ一つの部屋と同じくらい密接に、家の一部なのです——アルヴァ・アールト
The garden belongs to our home just as much as any of the room. —— Alvar Aalto

バタフライ屋根の形はアールト好み。壁はレンガのテクスチャーが透けた石灰塗り。ペンキと違い、経年変化で独特のテクスチャーを生みだす

The butterfly-shaped roof was one of Aalto's favorite styles. The wall is limewashed, showing the texture of the brick. Unlike paint, limewash brings out a distinctive texture that changes with the passage of time.

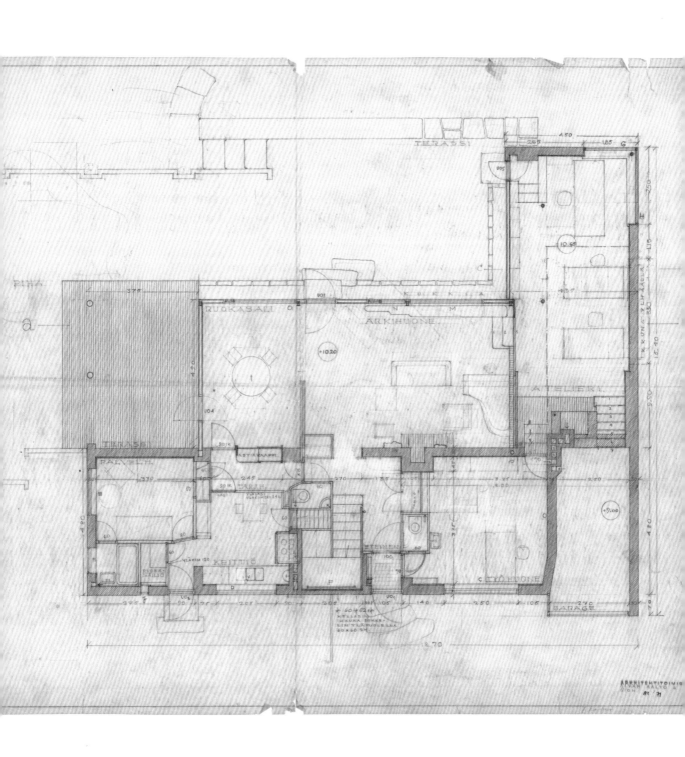

建設当初の1階平面図。鉄筋コンクリートと鉄骨の混構造で、庭側を鉄骨にして軽くし、窓を大きく開けている

Plan of the first floor when first built. Combining reinforced concrete and steel-frame for the structure, he used steel-frame for the garden side for a lighter effect, opened up with large windows.

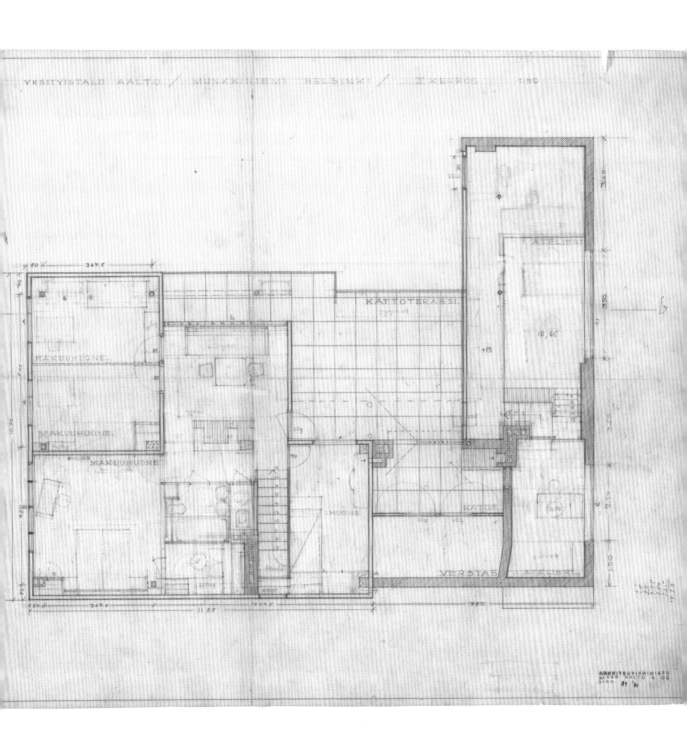

2階平面図。ルーフテラスを中央にして、左に住居、右に仕事場。仕事場からも直接テラスへ出られる

Plan of the second floor. The roof terrace is in the center, flanked by the living quarters on the left and the studio on the right, both with direct access to the terrace.

リビングルーム。すべてのディテールを簡素化した上でつくられたソフトな部屋の雰囲気
Living room. The room has a gentle atmosphere created by the simplification of all the details.

秋の西日で満たされたリビングルーム。ここは仕事場と隣接し、応接室も兼ねる

Living room filled with the evening sun in autumn. Adjacent to the studio, it doubles as a room for receiving guests.

昼過ぎからの光。ヘンリーツタの色で部屋に入射する光は季節の色合いを帯びる

Light of the afternoon. The light entering the room is tinted by the seasonal colors of the ivy on the walls.

リビングルームからダイニングルームを見る／梁を最小限の細さにし、隠さず天井面に見せる
View from the living room toward the dining room. The roof beams are made as slender
as possible and left exposed on the ceiling.

ダイニングルーム。庭の景を大きく取りこむ。こげ茶色の壁は布地張り。椅子は1924年の新婚旅行の際にイタリアで求めたもの

Filled with the vista on the garden, the dining room's dark-brown wall covered with fabric. The chairs were purchased on the architect's honeymoon to Italy in 1924.

階段の踊り場から見る
View from the landing of the stairs.

2階のファミリールーム。煙突は暖炉の正面をずらし、廊下にはトップライトを取る

Second story family room. The chimney is offset from the center of the fireplace.
The top light illuminates the corridor.

2 階のベッドルーム。朝日がふんだんに差しこむよう、東側に窓を取る

Second floor bedrooms, with windows on the east side to bring in the bright morning sun.

（上）吹き抜けになった仕事場には、大きな高窓から西日が差しこむ
（左）奥の窓をL形にし、庭との親密感を高める
（左頁）仕事場から図書室へ。暖炉の上部に階段。中2階のバルコニーへ通じる

(Above) The studio has a ceiling open to the second floor and a large, tall window facing west.
(Left) The window is L-shaped, heightening the sense of closeness with the garden.
(Opposite page) From the studio, looking toward library, the stairway over the fireplace, and the passage to the balcony on the mezzanine floor.

Aalto House & Studio

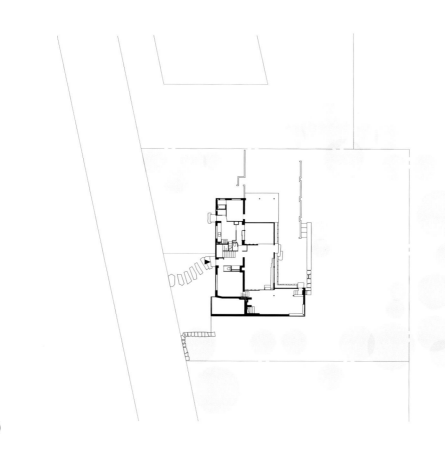

After completing the Paimio Tuberculosis Sanatorium in the summer of 1933, Aalto moved his office that fall from Turku to Helsinki. Work on the Viipuri City Library, a project for which he had won the competition in 1927, had, after various complications, finally begun to move forward. Even Helsinki was closer to Viipuri (at the time part of Finnish territory; today the Russian city of Vyborg) 200 kilometers to the east, where he would be supervising progress on this major project.

In 1935, Aalto purchased land in the residential community of Munkkiniemi about five kilometers northwest of central Helsinki. The site of about 1,350 square meters slopes slightly in the direction of the sea to the south. This house is the first work indicating Aalto's break with functionalism and displaying his own ideas about architecture. Leaving behind the abstract forms of "white architecture" he chose materials evoking a sense of warmth and made the most of their various textures. Many of the approaches to this work, including his preference for original resolutions to the site environment and introduction of details deriving from his accumulated experience, are ones that became the basis of later works and developed further from there.

The street runs along the site at a slight diagonal to the front side of the house, truncating one side of the lot. This creates a perspective view as one approaches from the street and confronts the large white wall of the house, which looks wider than in reality. The proportions of the windows and doors on the street side of the house are restrained, forming a facade that is closed to the townscape. The black and white volumes assert a striking contrast, the black parts the living quarters walled with vertical siding and the white parts the studio area with limewashed brick.

The real front of this house is not the street facade but the side facing the garden beyond. Regarding the orientation of dwellings on a site, Aalto would later state: "the road must be at the back and the facade must face the garden."[10] Following this conviction, the street-side facade is simple and closed, while that on the garden side blossoms with expressions of openness. The wall of the central portion with the living and dining rooms is made up of large fixed-pane windows and the terrace is above. Various elements are added to mediate the lines

ヴィープリの図書館
Viipuri City Library (1927−35).

1933 年の夏、パイミオのサナトリウムを完成させると、その秋にアールトは事務所をトゥルクからヘルシンキへ移した。折しも1927 年にコンペで獲得したヴィープリの図書館が、敷地の変更などの紆余曲折を経てようやく本格的に動きだしていた。ヘルシンキからヴィープリ（旧フィンランド領で、現在はロシア領ヴィボルグ市）まで東へ 200km ほどの距離のため、この大きなプロジェクトの進行監理も移転の理由の一つだった。

　アールトは1935 年、ヘルシンキ中心部から 5km ほど北西の住宅地ムンキニエミに土地を購入した。広さは 1351㎡、南の海方面へ向かって下がった傾斜地である。この家は、アールトが機能主義の影響から脱皮し、みずからの建築への考えを示した最初の作品といわれる。抽象的な「白い建築」を抜けだし、木やレンガなど、温かみのある素材を選択し、そのテクスチャーを前面に打ちだした。さらには、敷地環境への個別の解決法や、経験の蓄積から導きだした細やかなディテールなど、ここで試みられたアプローチの多くが、のちの作品の母体となり発展していく。

　敷地は玄関側に道路が斜めに走っており、台形のような形態となっている。そのため、道路から近づくと白壁の大きなヴォリュームに向かってパースペクティブがつき、見え方に伸びを感じさせる。道路側のファサードは、窓や扉など開口部のプロポーションに抑制を効かせ、町並みに対しては閉じた構えとなっている。黒いヴォリュームと白いヴォリュームのコントラストが歯切れよく強調されているが、黒の部分は縦の羽目板張りで住居部分、白い部分はレンガに石灰塗りで仕事場となっている。

　この家の「表」の顔は道路側ではなく庭側にある。アールトはのちに、敷地に対して住宅をどう配置するかについて、「通り側へは背中を向け、中庭側へ家の顔を向けるべき[10]」と述べている。その言葉どおりに、この住宅では控えめな道路側のファサードとは対照的に、庭側は開放的で表情に富む。リビングルームとダイニングルームのある中央部の壁面は大きな嵌め殺しのガラス窓で、その上はテラスになっている。窓の周囲には、トレリスをつくって壁面に植物を絡めたり、2階のテラスでは丸太の欄干やブリーズソレイユをつけたりして、外と内とを取りもつ緩衝的なエレメントを加えている。一方で、寝室がある黒い木造部分や、仕事場の白い壁面は開口を抑えて閉じ、中央に大きく開いた窓を挟むかたちにしている。庭側のファサードの魅力は、ただ庭に向かって開放するのではなく、この絶妙な壁面の開閉バランスにあり、さらには、建物と植物との密な絡みあい、遠近感をつくりだすよう配置された植栽などのランドスケーピングにある。

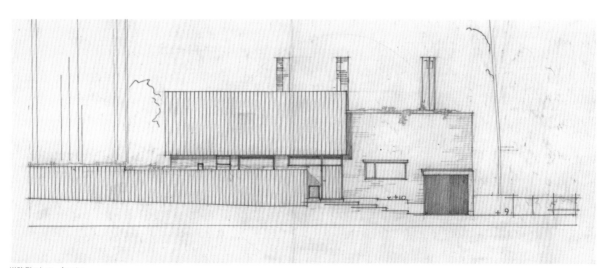

道路側エレベーション
Elevation to the street.

between inside and outside, including trellises affixed around the windows to encourage climbing vines, the log railing, and the brise-soleil over the terrace. The dark and wooden portions of the bedrooms and the white walls of the studio, meanwhile, are closed,* with few openings, flanking the large windows opening wide to the outside in the center. What gives the garden facade its appeal is not simply its openness to the outside, but the striking balance achieved between openings and wall surface, the literal intertwining of the building and the vegetation, and landscaping using plants, stone wall and other features that evoke an impression of distance.

The atmosphere of the interior is comfortable and intimate. The windows of the living and dining rooms give a full view of the garden, creating continuity between inside and outside. The foliage entwining the exterior trellises creates a green and red "curtain" that mingles light and color, bringing the space vividly to life. The dining room, living room, and studio are designed as one large continuous space, with the studio floor raised 45 centimeters above the other rooms, partitioned off with sliding wooden doors.

Details reflecting the Aaltos' ideas about quality and functionalism in everyday life can be found throughout this design. The interior combines materials with diverse textures to create an overall atmosphere of softness using cloth and wood, fabric woven of bark fiber, limewashed brick, and so on. At the same time, certain structural components are displayed as design elements, such as the three slender beams extending over the ceiling of the living area and the steel load-bearing post standing unadorned in one of the second-floor bedrooms. This method of combining traditional materials with manufactured products for their contrasts and harmonies is even more fully demonstrated in the later designed Villa Mairea.

Aalto lived in this house for 40 years until his death in 1976. As the years went by, the studio proved too small. In the mid-1950s, he built the Alvar Aalto Studio at a location about a five-minute walk away.

2階テラス
Second-floor terrace.

秋、リビングルームの窓辺
Living-room window in autumn.

内部は心地よい親密な空気に満ちている。1階のリビングルームとダイニングルームの窓からは庭の景色がいっぱいに広がっており、内から外へ連続感をつくりだしている。外壁のトレリスを這う葉は、緑や赤い「カーテン」となって内部空間に光と色を添え、生命感を与えている。ダイニング・リビング・仕事場は、連続感のある一つの大きな空間としてとらえられており、床を少し上げた仕事場は木の引き戸で仕切るようになっている。

　ここではアールト夫妻が生活に求めたクオリティ、機能性への意識がすみずみのディテールにまで行きとどいている。インテリアには布や木、樹皮繊維を平織りに編んだもの、石灰塗りのレンガなど、質感のある素材を組みあわせ、全体にソフトな雰囲気をつくりだしている。その一方で、リビングエリアに渡した3本の細身のコンクリート梁を天井面に隠さず部屋に露出させたり、2階では鉄パイプの構造柱を寝室にそのまま立てたりして、工業製品である構造部材をデザイン要素として見せている。伝統的な素材と工業製品とを組みあわせ、それらを対比させつつ調和する手法は、こののちに設計したヴィラ・マイレアで十二分に発揮される。

　アールトは1976年に亡くなるまで、ここに40年間住んだ。仕事場は手狭になり、1950年代半ばには、ここから徒歩で5分ほど離れた場所にアルヴァ・アールト・スタジオを建てている。

リビングルームから仕事場を見る
View from the living room toward the studio.

1930年代中頃のアールト事務所
Aalto studio in the mid 1930s.

アールト夏の家
Aalto Summer House
Muuratsalo, Finland (1952－1953)

パイヤンネ湖に浮かぶムーラッツァロ島の突端に立つ

The house stands on the western tip of Muuratsalo Island off the Päijänne lake shore.

ボートで湖からアクセスする。船着き場から岩山を登ると、木々の間から白壁が見えてくる

Access is by boat from the lake. Climbing up the rocks from the dock, the white walls of the house loom up among the trees.

光によって際立つ壁のテクスチャー
The light brings out the texture of the wall.

モニュメンタルなスケール感の白壁を手つかずの森のなかに挿入する。囲うことへの強い意識

White walls of monumental scale rise up within the untouched forest, witness of a strong impulse to enclose.

正面ファサード。南西に面する。白壁の内側は壁も中庭の床も赤レンガ

The front facade faces southwest. The inside is all red brick, both walls and floor of the courtyard.

美しい自然のなか、中庭で火を囲み、友人と過ごすのがこの家のコンセプト。50種類のレンガやタイルが床や壁にパッチワークのようにして使われている

The key concept of this house set in the midst of a beautiful landscape is a place to spend time with friends gathered around the fire in the courtyard. The walls and pavement feature a patchwork of 50 different textures of brick and tile masonry.

リビングルームから湖を見る。冬は壁の真向こうに夕日が沈む

The main window of the living room looks out on the lake, with a direct view of the setting sun in winter.

(左) リビングルームは吹き抜けで上階に小さなアトリエがある。太い柱や梁を使わず、最小限の寸法の部材で組みたてた簡素な工法
(上) 暖炉は幾何学的なプロポーションで、空間全体の印象を引き締めている

(Left) The living room has a ceiling open to the roof with a small loft-like atelier. The structure is minimal, without any large posts or beams, crafted in a pleasingly simple method.
(Above) The geometrically drawn lines of the fireplace set the tone of the entire space.

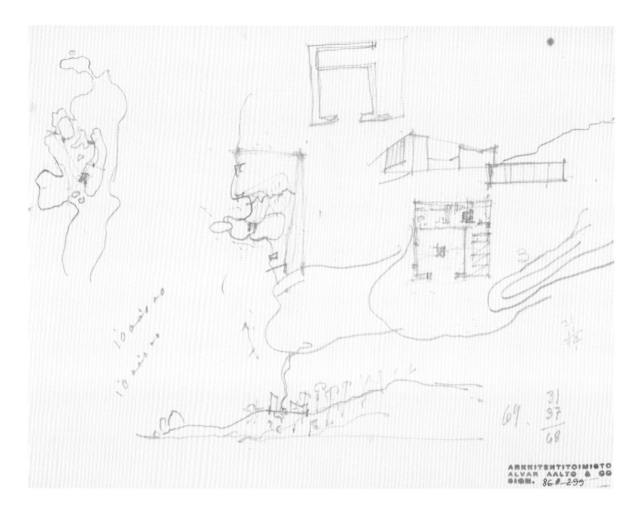

（上）下部には湖から見たスケッチがあり、林のなか、壁の間隙から煙が上がっている。家のコンセプトを考える段階で、アールトの頭のなかではすでに中庭の炉の火が燃えている。その上には簡単なプランとエレベーションのスケッチ。プランの形は完全な正方形を微妙に崩しており、このプロポーションのまま建設されていったのが右ページの平面図と比較するとわかる

（右上）断面図（上）とプラン（下）。中庭をL形に囲んだ母屋に木造のゲストルームが連結し、少し間隔を置いて物置小屋がある

（右下）南東側。内部にはベッドルームがある。道路側からは林を抜けてこの面からアクセスする

(Above) A sketch of the silhouette of the island seen from the lake at the bottom shows the walls of the house, with smoke rising up between them. Already at the concept stage, Aalto had the image of a fire burning in the courtyard in his head. Above that are sketches of the plan and elevation. The plan is an almost regular square, with one part open. The proportions of the final building are, as we can see from the plan on the right page, almost exactly as envisions in that sketch.

(Top right) Section (top) and floor plan (bottom). The wood-structure guest quarters is linked to the L-shaped main house, and, separated by a small space, the shed stands.

(Bottom right) The bedrooms are lined up along the southeast side. Access to the house from the road is from this side.

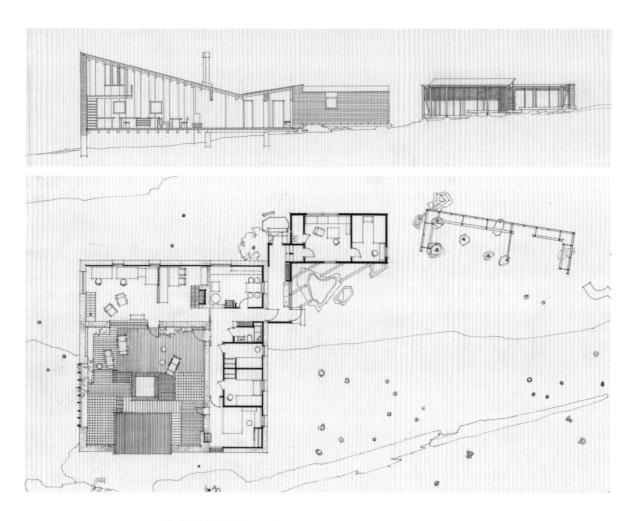

北東側。１年を通してこの壁面に直射光が当たるのは午前中の20分間

Northeast side. This wall receives direct sunlight for only 20 minutes during the morning throughout the year.

北側。垂直の木々のなか、風景に切りこむように斜めの屋根ラインが走る
North side. The roofline asserts a diagonal slash through the straight lines of the trees.

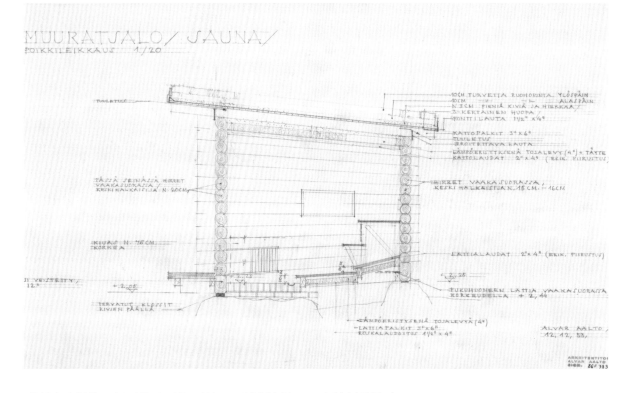

MUURATSALO / SAUNA /
POIKKILEIKKAUS 1/20

母屋から森の小道を30メートルほど北へ行った湖のほとりに、アールトは昔ながらのスモークサウナ小屋を建てた
On the bank of the shore 30 meters down a wooded path from the main house, Aalto built a traditional-style smoke sauna hut.

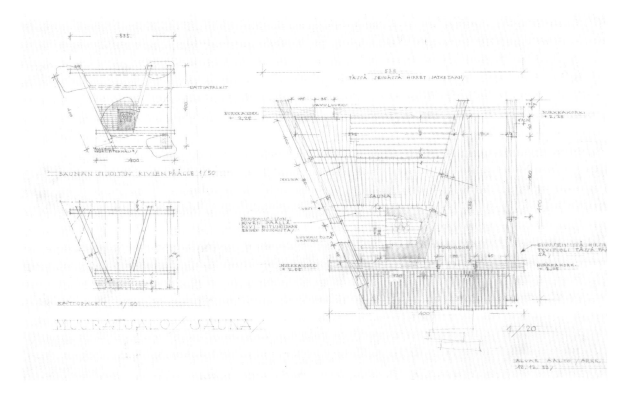

サウナのプランは台形。ストーブ上に石を積み置き、薪をくべて石を温めて小屋の温度を上げる

The plan of the sauna is a trapezoid. The heat of the hut is maintained by heating stones with a wood fire.

Aalto Summer House

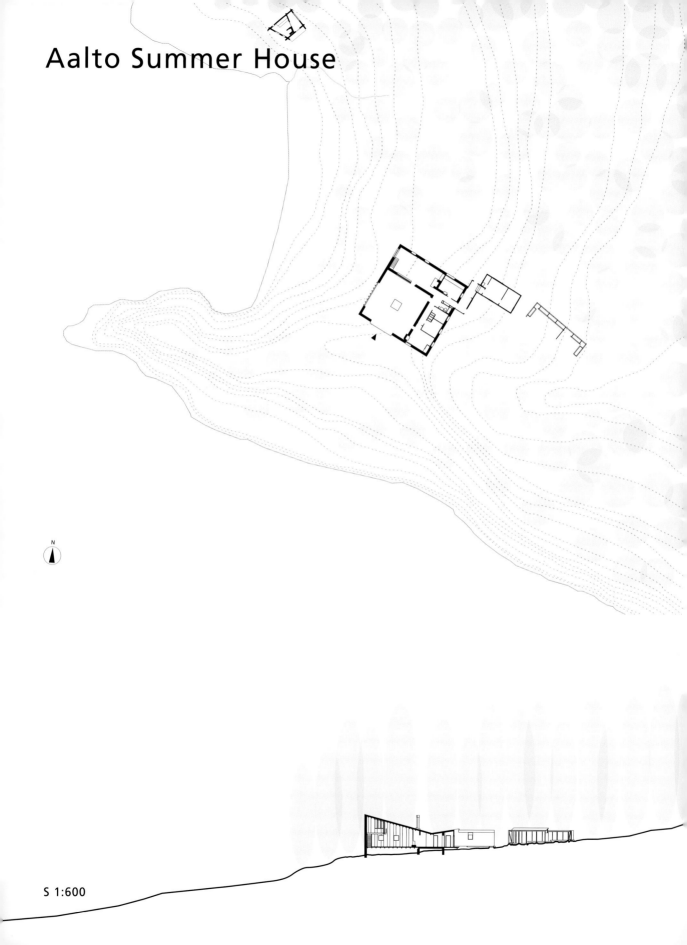

This cottage is on Muuratsalo, an island on a lake about 20 kilometers south from the center of Jyväskylä, Finland, some 4 kilometers south of the Säynätsalo Town Hall. Aalto found the property while he was designing and building the town hall and purchased the lot from Ahlström Co., the owners. The site is indeed outstanding, with granite boulders protruding from the earth and gently undulating topography. The lake exquisitely reflects the beauties of the sunset, and in the distance to the northwest one can see the Muurame Church, which Aalto designed while still in his twenties.

The usual entry to the cottage is via a meandering path through the woods leading from the main road on the southeast side, which is actually the back of the house. The basic premise of the design is access to the property by boat form the lake, so the front facade is the southwest side facing the lake. Crossing the lake south from Jyväskylä, the first sign of the cottage is the white walls and grillwork of the enclosure. With due respect to the landscape, here Aalto sought to build a structure that would look beautiful when viewed from the lake. These external walls built in his favorite medium of limewashed brick rise some eight meters on the north side, projecting the monumentality of the building on a bold scale. The white walls are inserted into the greenery of the forest to striking effect.

After the end of World War II, during Finland's reconstruction period in the 1940s and 1950s, Aalto won contracts for the design of numerous large-scale public buildings, so his designs gradually acquired a kind of monumentality. His works of this period employed red brick so often that they constitute an interlude that could be called his "red period." Beginning with the Baker House Senior Dormitory at the Massachusetts Institute of Technology (1946–49), and continuing with the Säynätsalo Town Hall (1948–52), the National Pensions Institute (1948–57), the Helsinki University of Technology (1949–66), the Jyväskylä Pedagogical Institute (1951–59), and the House of Culture (1952–58), he contributed to society through numerous projects and in all of these he used red brick.

For this summer house, a private dwelling built for himself during this period, there was no particular need to make a formal statement, yet its concept is at base the same as for the large-scale projects he was involved in at the time. A feature of this work is its varied rooflines.

ムーラメの教会
Muurame Church (1926–29).

セイナッツァロの役場
Säynätsalo Town Hall (1948–52).

この別荘は、ユヴァスキラの中心から南へ20km、湖に囲まれたムーラッツァロ島にある。セイナッツァロの役場から4kmほど南下した場所である。アールトはこの役場を設計・建設中に、アールストローム社が所有していたこの土地を気に入って売ってもらう。たしかにここは抜群の敷地である。花崗岩の巨岩が隆起し、土地の形状は起伏に富む。湖にはうっとりするような美しい夕焼けが映りこみ、しかも北西側の遠方には、アールトが20代のときに建てたムーラメの教会が望める。

一般に、今では道路と通じている南東側の森の小道を通ってこの別荘に入るが、この面は裏にあたる。本来は湖からボートでアクセスするのを前提に設計されており、正面ファサードは湖に向いた南西側となる。ユヴァスキラから湖を南下し、まず見えてくるのが格子の入った白壁である。ここでアールトは風景に敬意を払い、湖から見て美しい建築をつくろうとしている。レンガに石灰を塗った外壁は、北側の面では高さ8mほどあり、堂々としたスケール感はモニュメンタルな感じすらある。緑のなかにこの白壁を挿しこんだ効果は計り知れない。

戦後、1940年代から50年代のフィンランド復興期にあって、アールトはつぎつぎと大規模で公共的な機関の設計を獲得していき、おのずと作品はモニュメンタルな性質を帯びていった。また、この頃の作品については、「赤の時代」と形容されるほど赤レンガを使ったものが多い。アメリカのマサチューセッツ工科大学の学生寮ベーカーハウス (1946−49) を皮切りに、セイナッツァロの役場 (1948−52)、国民年金会館 (1948−57)、ヘルシンキ工科大学 (1949−66)、ユヴァスキラ大学 (1951−59)、文化の家 (1952−58) など、アールトは大きな社会的貢献を求められるプロジェクトに取りくみ、これらの外壁には赤レンガを使っている。

そんな時期に建てられたアールト自身のための夏の別荘は、肩肘張らないプライベートな建物ではあるが、コンセプトでは同時期に進行していた大規模プロジェクトと根を同じくしている。特徴的なのは、屋根の変化である。それまでの陸屋根から、戦後は鋭角に空を切るような屋根のラインを求めている。この別荘では、北側を高くして急勾配をつけたバタフライ屋根で、この形態は、住宅ではメゾン・カレ、ヴィラ・シルツへと発展していく。

基本的なプランは、一辺が約14m角のほぼ正方形で、白壁のなかに赤レンガ敷きの正方形の中庭を取り、それを囲んで母屋をL形に配している。中庭の中央には炉をつくり、火をおこして暖を取ったりバーベキューしたりできるようになっている。そもそもなぜこれほど風光明媚な場所の、湖に面した高台の突端の敷地にあって、周囲を壁で囲ってしまうのか。ここではリビングルームからの眺めを、額縁に収まった一幅の絵のように切りとろうと意図したわけでもなさそうだ。むしろ

ユヴァスキラ大学
Jyväskylä Pedagogical Institute (1951−59).

Moving away from the flat roof, after the war, he sought rooflines that formed sharp lines against the sky. The summer house has a butterfly roof sloping sharply upward to the north, a form that he later developed further in the Maison Carré and Villa Schildt.

The basic plan is a square of approximately 14 meters on a side. Within the white walls, the square courtyard is paved with red brick and the main house forms an L-shape at its back. In the center of the courtyard is a fireplace where visitors can warm themselves and where barbecues can be prepared. One may well wonder why the house, situated in a place with such a splendid view of the lake on a ridge overlooking the water, should be surrounded by a high wall. The idea of creating a kind of frame with which to capture the scene from the living room does not seem to be the real reason. Rather, one is struck with Aalto's apparently strong impulse for enclosure. Why would he want to close up space in such an extraordinary location?

The premise upon which this summer house was designed seems to have been that he would spend time here not alone, but with others in the courtyard. Aalto was incorporating intimate courtyards like this in other buildings, including preceding the Säynätsalo Town Hall and the later National Pensions Institute. He saw the courtyard as a place where people gather and spend time together as well as a centripetal space for tying together a variety of architectural elements.

There seem to have been several reasons why Aalto himself called his summer house *koetalo* (experimental). The first is that, in the design of a wood-constructed guest quarters placed on an extended straight line from the east side, he made natural boulders the foundations. As far as elements that would make the house qualify as experimental even today, one is certainly the variety of red brick and tile textures used for the walls surrounding the courtyard. Some 50 different types of brick and tile are said to have been used to cover the walls and ground in patchwork-like designs. No doubt these include many that were left over or excluded in the construction of the Säynätsalo Town Hall project nearby. Perhaps more than an experiment it is the project of Aalto's fondness for—or homage to—red brick.

The interior of the house is spare and practical. On the north side of the living room where the ceiling is at its highest, he hung a small room which he used as an atelier for painting. The

セイナッツァロの役場の中庭
Courtyard of Säynätsalo Town Hall.

印象的なのは、アールトの「囲う」ことへの強いこだわりであろう。このような絶好の地にあって、アールトは空間を「閉じる」。なぜなら、ここは一人で過ごす家ではなく、中庭で誰かと共に火を囲んで過ごす時間を想定してつくられた家だからである。アールトはこの住宅に先行するセイナッツァロの役場をはじめ、のちの国民年金会館でも密度のある中庭をつくっている。人が集い、共に過ごす場として、さらには、さまざまな建築的要素を一つに束ねる求心的な空間として中庭を位置づけようとしている。

この別荘をアールト自身が「実験住宅」(koetalo) と呼んだのには、いくつか理由があったようだ。たとえば、東側に直線上に延びる木造のゲストルームの設計で、自然の岩の上に土台を直接置く構造などである。今でも実験住宅という言葉に当てはまる要素があるとすれば、それは中庭を囲む壁面にさまざまなタイプの赤レンガやタイルを使った点だろう。ここでは50種類のレンガやタイルが選ばれているという。それをパッチワークのようにして壁や床に張っている。当然そのなかには、近くのセイナッツァロの役場の建設時に撥ねられたもの、余剰として出たものが多く混じっていただろう。これは実験というよりも、アールトの赤レンガへの愛着、オマージュである。

内部空間は簡素で歯切れがよい。リビングルームの北側、天井が高くなった層には木造の小部屋が吊ってあり、ここはアールトが絵を描くためのアトリエになっている。さりげないつくりだが、大きな柱や梁を使わずに、最小限の寸法の部材だけで吊った軽快で小気味よい工法である。

森のなかの小道を北側へ30mほど歩いた湖の畔に、アールトは伝統工法でサウナ小屋を建てた。薪で暖め、煙突をつけない古式なスモークサウナである。サウナのあとは湖へ。フィンランド人が培ってきた自然との一体感を、この建築家もこよなく愛したのであろう。

ダイニングルーム
Dining room.

中庭の赤レンガ壁
Courtyard surrounded with the red brick walls.

structure is minimal, without using any large posts or beams, using instead a pleasingly simple method for installing a small workspace with a minimum of timbers.

On the edge of the lake a 30-meter walk along a path through the woods on the north side, Aalto built a traditional-style sauna hut. It is an old-style wood-burning, smoke sauna without a chimney. After steaming in the sauna, one plunges directly into the lake. We can tell that this architect loved the oneness with nature that the Finns so wisely cultivated.

1960年代、ギーディオン夫妻たちと過ごすアールト夫妻
Aaltos with their friends, including Giedions, in the 1960s. Photo by Federico Marconi.

ヴィラ・オクサラ
Villa Oksala
Korpilahti, Finland (1965－1966・1974)

無人島に立つ夏の別荘。船で渡る
The summer cottage built on an uninhabited island is accessed by boat.

西日を受ける玄関側
Entrance side of the house bathed in the western sun.

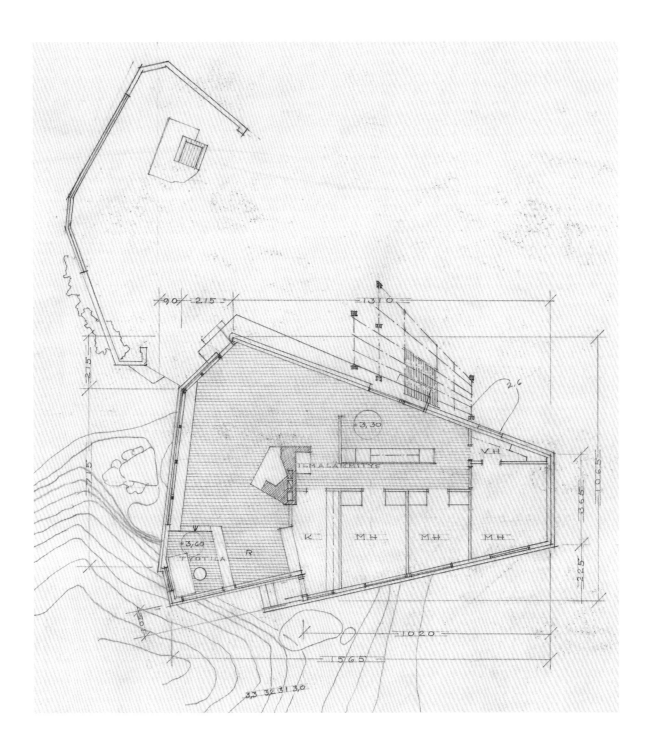

(左上) 南側ファサード　(左下) リビングルーム
(上) 平面図。南へ向けて裾広がりになった細い台形。南西側に石積みで囲った庭があり、リビングから直接庭へ出られる扉がつく

(Top left) South side. (Bottom left) Living room.
(Above) Floor plan. A slender trapezoid shape, opening out toward the south. A courtyard surrounded by a stone wall extends from the southwest side. The living room has a door opening directly on the courtyard.

暖炉は家の象徴的な中心。鉤形プランで、折れ曲がった地点に斜めに設置する

The fireplace is the symbolic center of the house. This part follows an hook-shaped outline with the fireplace situated at an angle.

Villa Oksala

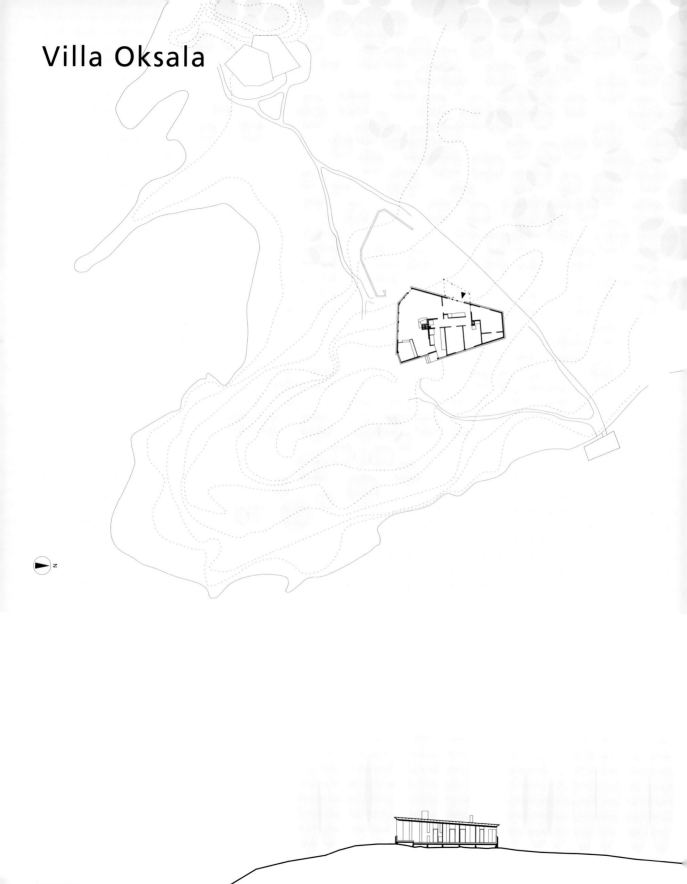

S 1:600

The Villa Oksala was built on an otherwise uninhabited island in a lake. The exclusively by-water approach is a 15-minute motor boat ride across Päijänne Lake, 40 kilometers south of Jyväskylä. Aalto did the design for his old friend, the linguist of classical languages Päivö Oksala, from 1965 to 1966, and it was built in 1974.

Nearing the island by boat, all that can initially be seen among the reeds are granite boulders and pine trees. Gradually one gets glimpses of the sauna hut near the water's edge and, rising over the rugged rocks reminiscent of the undulating back of a whale, the villa. Seen from the lake, the house blends in with its environment; in contrast with the white-painted walls used in his own summer home on nearby Muuratsalo island, for this house Aalto used materials and colors that assimilate it into its surroundings.

The exterior shows a clear distinction of materials for its upper and lower parts; the walls are wood and the foundations stone masonry using rocks from the island itself. Although a quite simple cottage, the cleanly defined roof details are impressive. The roof slants upward from the northern end and the eaves are lined with a double row of logs. The effect is reminiscent of the eaves treatment of traditional houses in the Finnish countryside, where people placed a layer of sod on their roofs to insulate against the cold in winter.

In plan, the house is like a partially closed fan opened out to the south side and tapering to the north. Judging from the drawings, a courtyard equipped with a fireplace and surrounded by a stone wall was planned for the southwest side. The door at the southwest corner of the living room must have been added for access to the courtyard.

The living area is opened wide toward the lake to the south through the windows. The fireplace is set on an angle and the living and dining rooms are set apart loosely, without any solid partition. The ceiling, made of wooden boards running in the direction of the roof's slope, unites the entire living area. Whether in a large and luxurious dwelling or a small log-cabin-style villa, the ceilings are invariably of special interest in Aalto's houses. Here, by spanning the ceiling in straight lines paralleling the slope of the roof, he unites the hook-shaped living area into a single space and gives it the feel of an expanse much larger than in reality.

小さな無人島に建てられた夏の別荘である。ユヴァスキラから40kmほど南下し、パイヤンネ湖上をモーターボートで走ること約15分、ここへ行きつくアクセスは水上しかない。アールトは旧友で古典言語学の教授パイヴォ・オクサラのために、この別荘を1965年から翌年にかけて設計した。建設されたのは1974年である。

　ボートから島へ近づくにつれ、葦の向こうにごつごつした花崗岩と松林が視界に入ってくる。まず、岸辺近くにサウナ小屋が、つぎに、鯨の背中のように隆起した大きな岩の上、林の合間から別荘が見え隠れする。湖からの見え方は、近くのムーラッツァロ島にあるアールトの夏の家が白塗り塀であるのに対し、ここでは周囲と同化する素材や色を使い、環境に建物を融けこませている。

　外壁の上部は木、下部は現地の石を野積みにし、素材を上下で明確に分けている。簡素な小屋でありながら、歯切れのよい屋根まわりのディテールが目を引く。勾配を北向きに下げた片流れ屋根で、短い庇の下、丸太を二重にまわしている。これは、屋根に土を載せて夏は草を生やし、冬はそれで断熱をした伝統的な民家の軒まわりのディテールに近い。

　プランはやや閉じた扇形をしており、南側を開き、北側に向かってすぼまっている。図面によると、当初南西側には石積みで囲った中庭をつくろうとしていたようで、火をおこす炉が描きこまれている。リビングルームの南西角には扉があるが、これは便宜上、その庭への出入りのために設けられたものであろう。

　リビングエリアは、湖に向けて南から東側をガラス窓で全面的に開いている。南側のコーナーには、床を少し上げて、5㎡ほどの小さな書斎をつくっている。格子やスクリーンでゆるやかに区切っただけのスペースだが、どこか楽しげな雰囲気のある魅力的な一角である。

　暖炉は斜めに設置され、リビングルームとダイニングルームの間は壁を立てずにゆるやかに区分けされている。東側、ダイニングの脇の窓からは湖の眺めが近く、水や風を身近に感じられる。天井は屋根勾配に沿って傾斜のついた板張りで、リビングエリア全体に統一して張られている。アールトの住宅では、大きな邸宅であろうと小さな丸太小屋風の別荘であろうと、天井は大きな魅力の一つである。ここでは天井をシンプルな直線の片流れにして張りわたすことで、鉤形に曲がったリビングエリアをシングルスペースにまとめ、実際の面積よりも広々とした空間をつくりだしている。

東側。丸太を二重にまわした軒のディテール
East side. Eaves detail with a double row of logs.

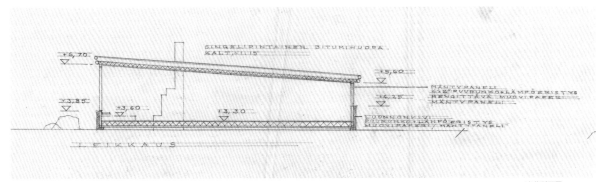

南北断面図
North-south section.

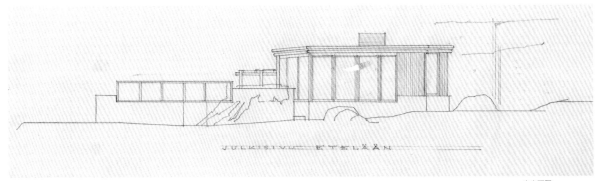

南立面図
South elevation.

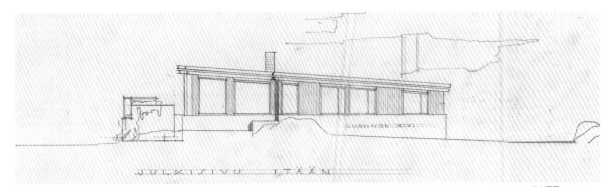

東立面図
East elevation.

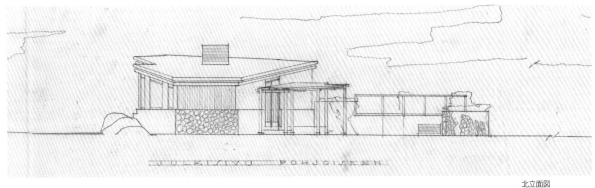

北立面図
North elevation.

ヴィラ・シルツ
Villa Schildt
Tammisaari, Finland (1969－1970)

庭とつながった公園の前に立ち、2階の窓が斜めに迫りだす
Built in front of a park on the edge of an inlet, the house features a window that protrudes on an angle on the second floor

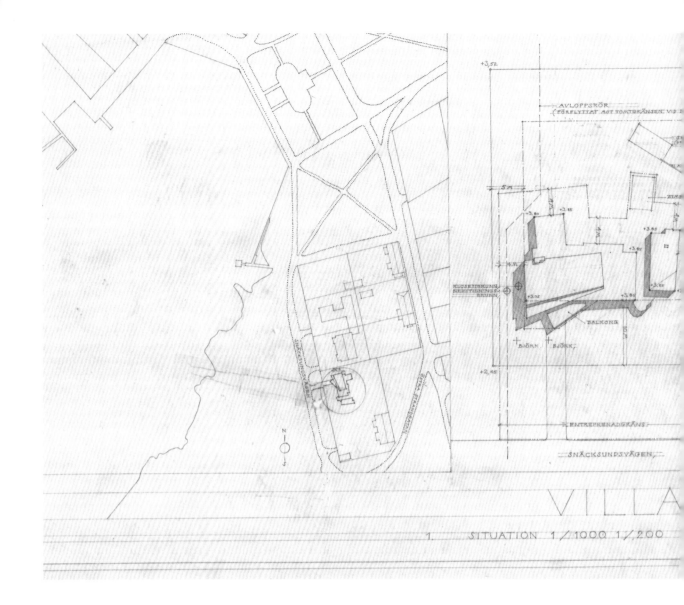

（上）配置図。1970 年 1 月 20 日。左の図では、入江の形や海を挟んだ北側の町とヴィラ・シルツとの距離感がわかる。道路に対して 1 階は平行に建て、2 階の窓とバルコニーを南西に突きだす。その真向こうには、葦の繁った水辺の風景がある
（右上）北側。スエーデン文化の影響が残る古い町並み
（右下）南西側。葦の生えた人為の入っていない美しい入り江

(Above) Site plans. January 20, 1970. The drawing on the left gives a sense of the shape of the inlet and the distance of the house from the town on the north across the water. The first floor is parallel to the street, but the second floor window and balcony project on an angle toward the southwest. Straight out the window is the view of the reed-filled shallows in the wild part of the inlet shore.
(Top right) View to the north. Old townscape where legacy of Swedish culture left its imprint.
(Bottom right) View to the southwest. Beautiful wild part of the inlet.

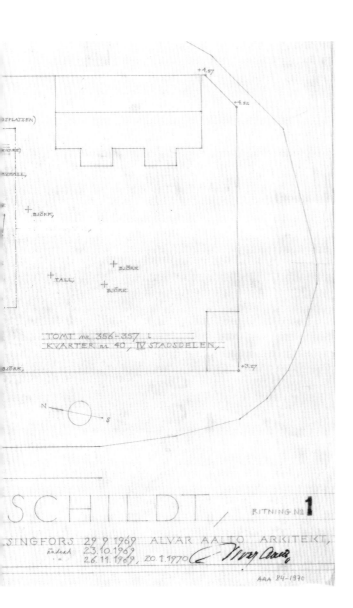

(GSPLATSEN)

+ BJÖRK,

+ TALL, + BJÖRK,
+ BJÖRK,

TOMT nr. 356-357 i
KVARTER m. 40, IV STADSDELEN,

BJÖRK,

N S

SCHILDT, RITNING N° 1

...SINGFORS 29.9.1969 ALVAR AALTO ARKITEKT,
ändrad 23.10.1969
'' 26.11.1969, 20.1.1970

AAA 84-1970

西側正面ファサード。異なる要素を組みあわせてまとめるアールトの巧みな指揮棒

The front facade on the west side demonstrates the skillful orchestration of diverse elements into a harmonious whole.

白と黒はアールトの基本色。正方形に近い二つの窓が全体を引き締める
White and black were Aalto's basic colors. The two nearly square windows sharpen the balance of the whole.

幾何学的な分割の白い壁とフリーフォームの格子の組みあわせ
View showing the white wall, with its geometric motifs, combined with the free form of the lattice.

北側・西側立面図　North and west elevations.

南側・東側立面図　South and east elevations.

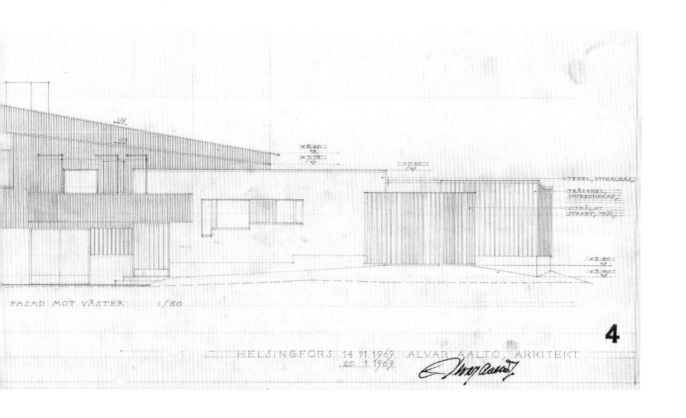

FASAD MOT VÄSTER   1/50

TEGEL, VITKALKAS,
TRÄPANEL IMPREGNEKAS
VITMÅLAT
STAKET, TRÄ,

4

HELSINGFORS 14.11.1969 ALVAR AALTO, ARKITEKT
20.1.1969

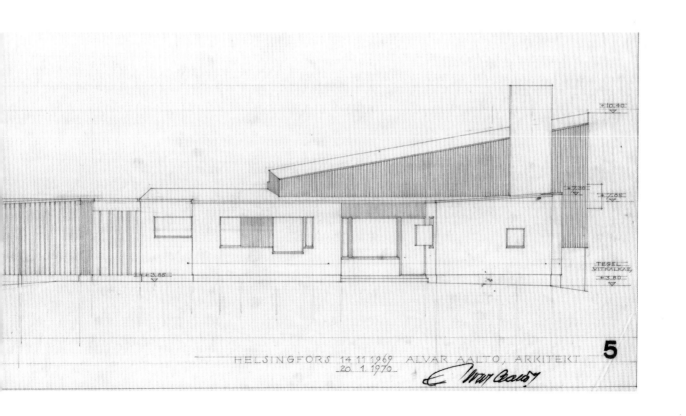

TEGEL
VITKALKAS,

5

HELSINGFORS 14.11.1969 ALVAR AALTO, ARKITEKT
20.1.1970

中庭に面する東側。書斎、ベッドルームがあり、大きな窓を開けて朝の光を室内に入れる

East side, facing the courtyard. The bedroom and study have large windows that bring in the morning sun.

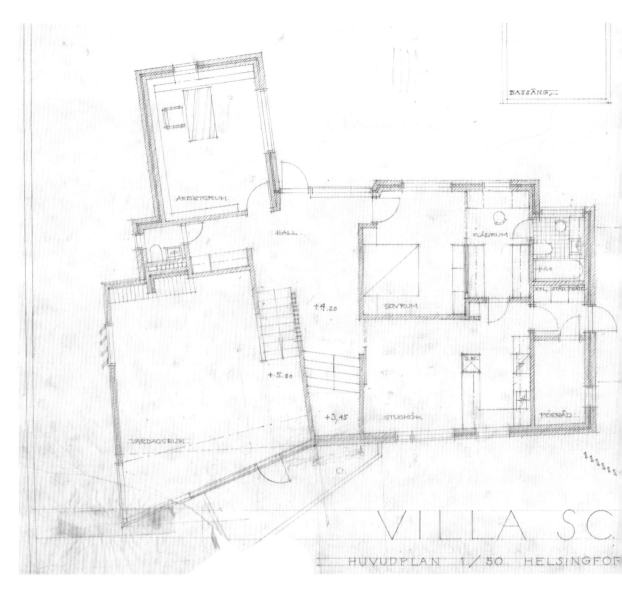

ARBETSRUM

HALL

KLÄDRUM

WC

KYL. STÄD. TVÄTT

+4.20

SOVRUM

+5.80

3.K.

+3.45

STUGKÖK

FÖRRÅD

VARDAGSRUM

BASSÄNG

VILLA SC

HUVUDPLAN 1/50 HELSINGFOR

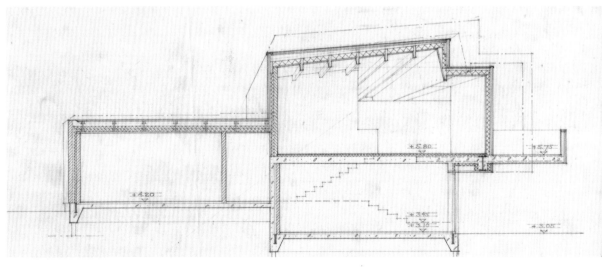

+5.80

+5.75

+4.20

+3.45

+3.10

+3.05

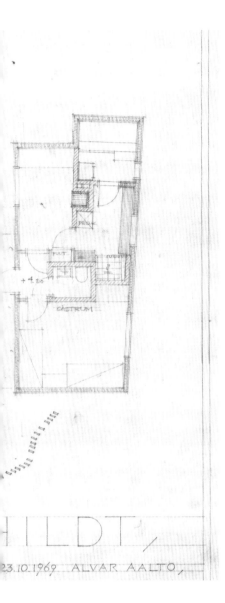

HILDT/

23.10.1969 ALVAR AALTO

（左）平面図。波状の格子は母屋と隣接した木造の離れをつないでいる。離れにはサウナとゲストルームがある
（下）断面図。1970 年1月20日付

(Left) Plan. The wavy lattice links the main house to the adjacent wood-structure cottage. The cottage houses the sauna and guest room.
(Below) Sectional drawings. Dated January 20, 1970.

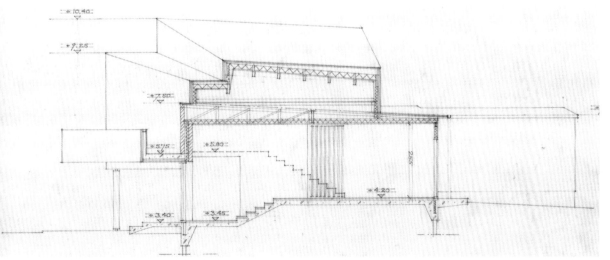

(左) 左奥に玄関。台形のホールは吹き抜けで、スキップフロアにして階高に変化をつけつつ玄関ホールと2階の空間を滑らかにつなげる
(上) この家の見所の一つは、小梁を見せた迫力ある天井

(Left) The wedge-shaped entrance hall is open to the second floor. The stairways give the split-level layout variety while connecting the entrance hall and the second-floor space in a fluid fashion.
(Above) The highlight of this house is the dynamic design of the ceiling.

2階リビングルーム。壁の高さに変化をつけ、吹き抜けホールとの一体感を強めた開放的な空間
Living room on the second floor. The stair-stepped wall heightens the unity of the space with the high-ceilinged entrance hall beyond.

夕日を受ける暖炉はアールトのデザイン
The evening sun shines onto the fireplace, by Aalto's design.

入江の眺めが広がる出窓。冬には日没が見られる　The bay window opens up the view toward the inlet, and, in winter, a clear view of the sunset.

Villa Schildt

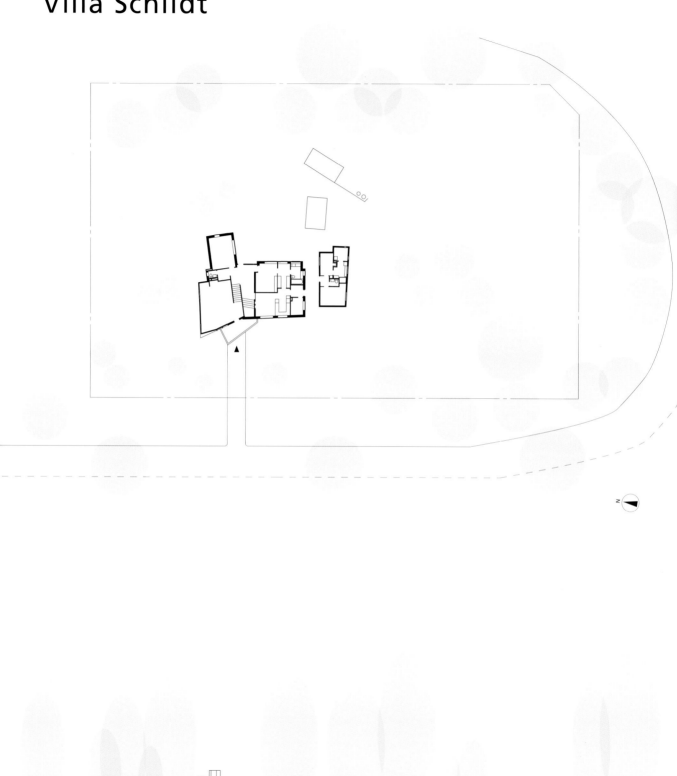

S 1:600

The house built for Aalto's close friend and biographer Göran Schildt and his wife Christine is located about 100 km west of Helsinki in Tammisaari, an old coastal town rich in Swedish-influenced traditions. The site faces a park across the street and 50 meters down the street, a beautiful inlet of the Baltic Sea. From the site one can see the yacht harbor and church steeples across the inlet and reed-filled shallows along the shore that preserve the natural beauty of the area.

Situated on a spacious site, there must have been no restrictions on the orientation of the plan, but Aalto made "southwest-facing" his theme. In other words the plan is keyed to the southwest not just for the light from that direction but for its view. The shoreline landscape to the southwest is completely unspoiled and also permits a view on clear winter days of the sunset. The concept sketch for this house has been preserved, showing that Aalto started with a rectangle parallel to the street, which he split in two. Then he set them apart and angled one side, as if bent toward the other, and this part is the second-story living room projecting at a diagonal toward the southwest. In the gap between the two parts is a wedge-shaped space conceived as an entrance hall with a ceiling open to the second floor that, in his mind, connects with the pond in the courtyard on the east side.

The plan shows the first-floor study and bedroom facing east with large windows facing the courtyard to greet the morning sun. The front door is at the street end of the entrance hall wedge. Going through the door and climbing up a flight of five steps, one sees the courtyard with the pond beyond through the glass window. On the second floor is the living room. The corner of the north wall is skewed 22.5 degrees to make the large picture window face southwest. Flanking the living room on the front side of the house is a small balcony also angled toward the southwest.

The living room is filled with a quiet light in the morning, but from afternoon, bright sun enters from the southwest and, reflected against the large white wall on the north side, fills the entire room with light. The attraction of the interior of this house is the dynamic design of its ceiling. The entrance hall is open to the second floor and the beams of the ceiling extend over both spaces (the hall and the living room upstairs). The beams are structural members running not east and west, but lengthways in the north-south direction following the slope of the roof.

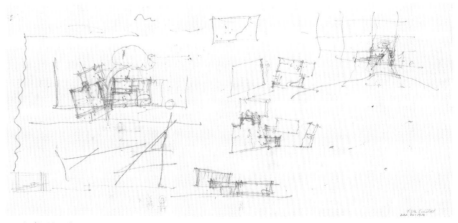

コンセプトスケッチ
Concept sketch.

アールトの近しい友人で彼の伝記作家でもあるヨーラン・シルツと妻クリスティーネのために設計された住宅である。場所はヘルシンキから西へ100kmほど、スエーデン文化の色濃く残る海岸沿いの古い町タンミサーリにある。敷地は、道路を挟んで前面に公園が広がり、そこから50mほど先には美しい入り江が広がっている。敷地近辺から見ると、湾の北側にはヨットハーバーや教会の鐘楼が望め、湾の南から西にかけては、葦の生えた自然のままの美しい水辺がある。

広々とした敷地にあって、アールトはこの家のテーマを「南西向き」に絞りこむ。つまり、南向きの光を最優先にするのではなく、眺めの方を設計の鍵にしている。南西方向には人為の入っていない水辺の景色があるし、冬には日没が眺められる。この家のコンセプトスケッチ（p.235）が残されているが、それによると、アールトはまず道路と平行に長方体を想定し、それを二つに割っている。つぎに、その二つを切り離し、一方を迫りだすようにして斜めに振っている。その部分が斜めに突きだした2階のリビングルームに相当する。そして、割った間隙にできた台形のスペースを玄関ホールにしており、それがアールトの意識のなかでは東側の中庭にある池とつながっている。

プランを見ると、1階の書斎、ベッドルームを東側に向け、朝日が入るように中庭に面して大きく窓を取っている。台形をした玄関ホールは、階段を5段上がると奥の中庭側へとガラス窓を通して視線が貫通する。2階にはリビングルームがあり、北側の角を22.5°振って大きなガラス窓を南西に向けており、その外側には、やはり南西に振った小さなバルコニーをつけている。

リビングルームには午後になると南西から光が差しこむ。その光は部屋の北側の白い壁面にあたり、部屋全体に光をまわす。この大きな壁面は、いわば反射板のような役割を果たしている。内部空間でこの住宅のいちばんの魅力は、迫力ある天井である。玄関ホールは吹き抜けになっており、天井の梁は玄関ホールとリビングルームの二つの空間を貫いて渡している。梁は家の東西方向ではなく南北方向の長手に、屋根の傾斜に合わせて架けてある。そのため空間にダイナミックな水平の伸びをつくりだし、開放感を高めている。

主屋の南側、少し離したところには木造の離れがつづく。なかはゲストルームとサウナである。主屋と離れとはキャノピーで連結し、その外側を波状の白い格子で囲って道路からの視線をゆるやかに遮断している。1階部分のガレージはコンクリート造、ダイニングやキッチン、ベッドルームのあるブロックは石灰塗りのレンガ造で、その上に木造を載せ、さらに木造の離れがつながる。これらの異なる要素を束ねているのが、玄関脇にある二つの正方形に近い窓である。すっきりした幾何学的な比例が使われており、この窓によって全体の印象が引き締められている。

玄関ホールから中庭を見る
View from the entrance hall to the courtyard.

夏の中庭
Courtyard in the summertime.

This design creates a dynamic horizontality, enhancing the openness of the space. In addition, these beams run perpendicular to the lines of movement in the house, placing their deep dimensions in view and thereby augmenting the sense of depth.

On the south side of the main house, separated by about two meters, is a wood-constructed cottage containing a guest room and sauna. The intervening space is covered with a canopy and partially screened from the street side with a wave-shaped white lattice.

The garage on the first floor is concrete with the wood-constructed living room section above it painted black. The block containing the dining room, kitchen, and bedroom is made of white limewashed brick. Beyond it stands the black structure of the cottage. Bringing together these disparate elements are the two rectangular windows to the side of the entrance way. With their clean-lined geometrical proportions, they sharpen the impression of the design as a whole.

玄関ホール、石灰塗りの壁。奥にはダイニングとキッチンがある
Limewashed wall in the entrance hall. Behind are the dining room and kitchen.

西に向いたダイニングルーム
Dining room facing the west.

ヴィラ・コッコネン

Villa Kokkonen
Järvenpää, Finland (1967—1969)

庭側。パーゴラはサウナ小屋へと導く
View from the garden. The pergola leads to the sauna hut.

南西に湖が見える小高い敷地にあって建物を三つのヴォリュームに分け、扇状に配置して南から西にかけて空間を開いている。中央にリビングルーム、一段高くなったヴォリュームには作曲家の仕事場がある

On a rise with a view of the lake through the trees to the southwest, the house is divided into three volumes that fan out from south to west. In the center is the living room. The slightly taller volume is the composer's studio.

玄関を入った地点。左が仕事場、右がリビングルーム

View of the interior from the entrance. At left is the studio; at right the living room.

仕事場からリビング方向を見る。内部全体がワンルームのようなコンセプト
This view from the studio toward the living room reveals the concept of the whole house as one room.

扉は鉛入りで、閉めると防音室に。吸音を施した天井の下に布を張り、残響を和らげる
The studio door is lined with lead, soundproofing the room when closed.

冬の午前中、南側の窓からの光。木々が葉を落とすと、南西方向に湖が見える。光の変化が豊かな南から西面の窓を幅の狭い連窓にし、室内に落ちる影にもリズムをつける

Light through the windows on the south during the morning in winter. The lake can be seen to the southwest in the wintertime. The south to west windows have been made a series of tall and narrow panes to create a rhythm of light and shadow within the room.

空間全体に柔らかな雰囲気を演出する暖炉。シラカバの床張りにトラヴァーチンの切り替えが波打ち際のように曲線を描いて走る

The fireplace imbues the entire space with an atmosphere of softness. The line between the white birch and travertine parts of the floor follows a wave-like curve.

西に向くリビングルーム。ツタの葉は季節の色を帯びた自然のカーテン。アールトの住宅では、内から外への推移は窓に這わせた植物が間を取りもつ

The living room faces west. Vines hanging down over the windows provide a natural curtain of foliage that changes color with the seasons. In Aalto's houses, plants climbing around the windows mediate the transition lines between interior and exterior.

(左) ダイニングルーム。トップライトからペンダントランプを吊る
(上) ダイニングからリビングを見る。まわる動線になっていて、空間は滑らかにつながっていく

(Left) In the dining room, pendant lamps hang from the skylight.
(Above) View from the dining room into the living room. This house has circular lines of movement and smooth transitions from one space to another.

Villa Kokkonen

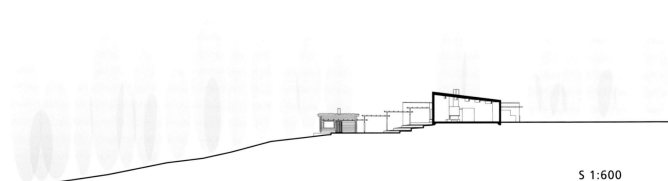

S 1:600

Joonas Kokkonen was a composer with whom Aalto became friends at the Academy of Finland. Kokkonen commissioned the design in 1967 and the two men went together to visit the site near the shore of Lake Tuusula about 40 kilometers north of Helsinki. When they stopped to eat on the way home, Aalto sketched his concept of the house on the restaurant tablecloth. The site slopes down in the western direction and is surrounded by trees on the south and west sides; the lake lies off to the southwest. The idea of positioning the front entrance on the east side at the road and giving the house a sweeping view of the lake from the south to the west probably came to him immediately after seeing the site.

In response to Kokkonen's request for a place where he could walk around a grand piano, Aalto conceived a house with a studio for the composer to absorb himself in his work with the grand piano as its centerpiece. The plan consists of three sections divided in a fan-like arrangement, the studio on the south, the dining room, kitchen, and bedrooms on the north, with the living room in between. The living room faces a courtyard on the western slope.

Roughly in the center of the house is a white, wave-shaped wall enclosing a washroom and cloakroom. Many of Aalto's designs incorporate angled lines that draw the line of vision diagonally, and the wave-shaped wall serves this purpose here and is the pivot of the design. Seen from the studio, the wall plays the role of divider, splitting the line of vision toward the living room to the left and corridor to the right, imparting a sense of space and perspective depending on the angle from which it is viewed.

The studio has a high ceiling and windows on the south and west sides. In winter, after the leaves have fallen from the trees, the room commands a view of Lake Tuusula to the southwest. With a sliding door lined with lead, the room is well soundproofed, allowing the composer to concentrate on his work. Small concerts were also occasionally held in this room.

One of the attractions of this house is its flow lines. Smooth lines of movement extend from entrance to the main space of the living and dining rooms, creating a flowing composition without stagnant areas, as if the living room and dining room were an integral part of the corridor. There is a door from the dining room opening on the courtyard, and a flight of steps under a pergola leads about 15 meters away to the guest room that serves also as an anteroom to the sauna.

玄関側
Front facade.

作曲家ヨーナス・コッコネンのために建てられた住宅である。アールトとコッコネンとはフィンランド芸術院を通して知りあい、友情を築いた。1967年に設計が依頼され、二人は一緒に敷地を見にいく。ヘルシンキから約40kmほど北へ行ったトゥースラ湖にほど近い場所である。その帰りに寄ったレストランで、アールトはテーブルクロスにこの家のコンセプトスケッチを描いた。敷地は西へ下がった傾斜地で、南側と西側は樹木に囲まれ、南西側には湖がある。道路の東側に玄関を配置し、そこから湖が見える南から西へ向けて家の空間を大きく開くアイディアは、敷地を見たとき、すぐにアールトの頭に浮かんでいただろう。

グランドピアノの周囲を歩きまわれるようにしてほしい、というのがコッコネンからのリクエストで、作曲活動にいそしむための仕事場、そこに置くグランドピアノを中心にこの家は設計された。プランは三つの部分に分かれた扇形で、南側にスタジオ、北側にダイニングルームとキッチン、ベッドルーム、中央にリビングルームを挟んだかたちである。

家のほぼ中央部には波形の白い壁面があり、背後には手洗いとコート掛けがあって、それを囲っている。アールトは空間のどこかに斜線を挿入し、斜めに視線を引っ張ることが多いが、ヴィラ・コッコネンではこの波形の壁がそれで、扇子でいうと要（かなめ）の部分に当たる。仕事場から壁の方向を見たとき、それはリビングルームへの眺めと廊下への眺めとに視線を分ける「ディバイダー」の役割をしており、角度をつけることで、空間の広がりや遠近感を巧みにつくりだしている。さらには、仕事場からリビング、廊下にかけて、木の床面をトラバーチンで曲線に切り替え、空間に奥行きをつくりだしている。

仕事場は天井を高くし、南側と西側に連窓を開けている。樹木が葉を落とす冬には、南西にトゥースラ湖を望める。音響面の配慮もあってか、天井にはキャンバス地の布を張っているが、この布は天井からの照明を和らげる効果もある。この部屋の引き戸にはなかに鉛が入っていて、いったん戸を閉めれば作曲に集中できるよう完全な防音室になる。ときにここで小コンサートが行われることもあったという。

この家の魅力の一つに、動線がある。玄関・リビング・ダイニングの主要空間は滑らかにまわる動線になっていて、廊下の一部に、あるいは、廊下のなかにリビングやダイニングがあるような、よどみのない流動的な構成である。ダイニングを特徴づけているのはトップライトで、そこからペンダント照明を吊っている。ダイニングからは中庭へ出る扉があり、パーゴラの下、15mほど階段を下りるとゲストルームを兼ねたサウナ小屋へとつづいている。

白い波形の壁
Wave-shaped wall.

滑らかにまわる動線
Smooth lines of movement from one space to another.

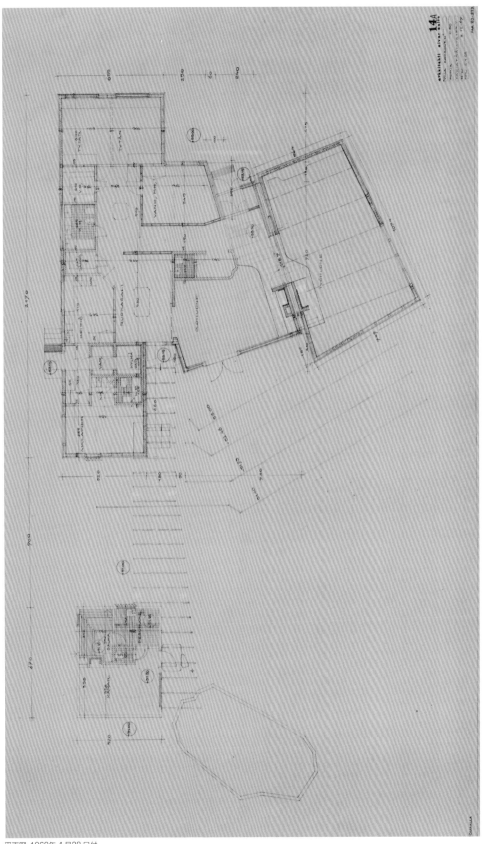

平面図。1968年 4 月28 日付
Plan. Dated April 28, 1968.

メゾン・アホ

Maison Aho

Rovaniemi, Finland (1964 – 1965)

西側。高さ制限のある分譲地に立つ

West side. The house was built in a housing district with restrictions on height.

正面ファサード。玄関は塀の奥にある。控えめなたたずまいのなかに、緊張感のある窓。アールトは当初、外壁を石灰塗りレンガにするつもりで建物のヴォリュームを考えていた

Front facade. The entrance is behind the exterior brick wall. Although the house is restrained in appearance, the window is striking. Aalto had planned the volume of the building in line with his original intention of using limewashed brick for the exterior.

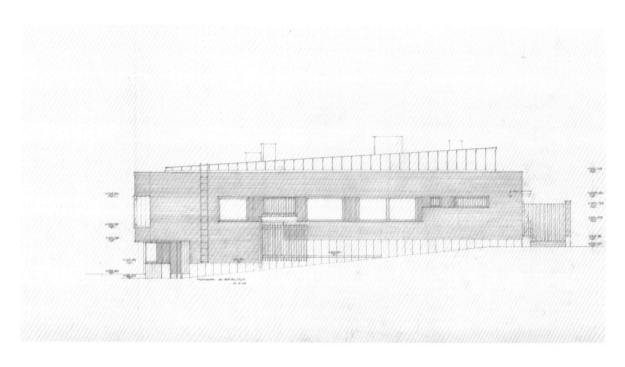

（左）東側。斜面を利用して2階建てにしている
（上）西側の窓まわり。オリジナルプランでは下階のこの部分にサウナがあり、庭への出入り口が設けられた

(Left) East side. The house is made two-story, utilizing the elevation of the slope.
(Above) Window treatment on the west side. In the original plan, there was a sauna on the lower floor of this part and a door was provided opening on the garden.

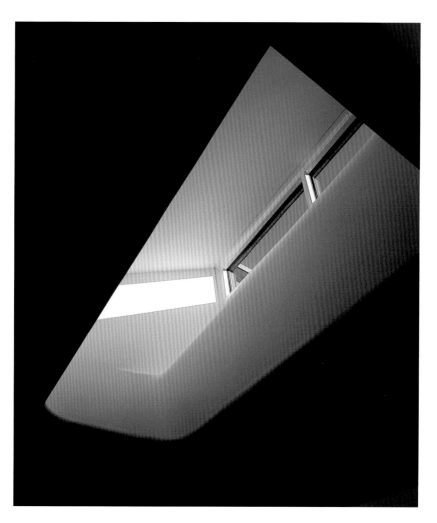

（左）玄関ホールからの眺め。奥のダイニングの窓まで一気に20m視線が貫通する
（上）夏の早朝にはトップライトから直射光が入る

(Left) The view from the entrance hall extends all the way to the dining room windows 20 meters through the house.
(Above) In the early morning in summer, direct light enters through the skylight.

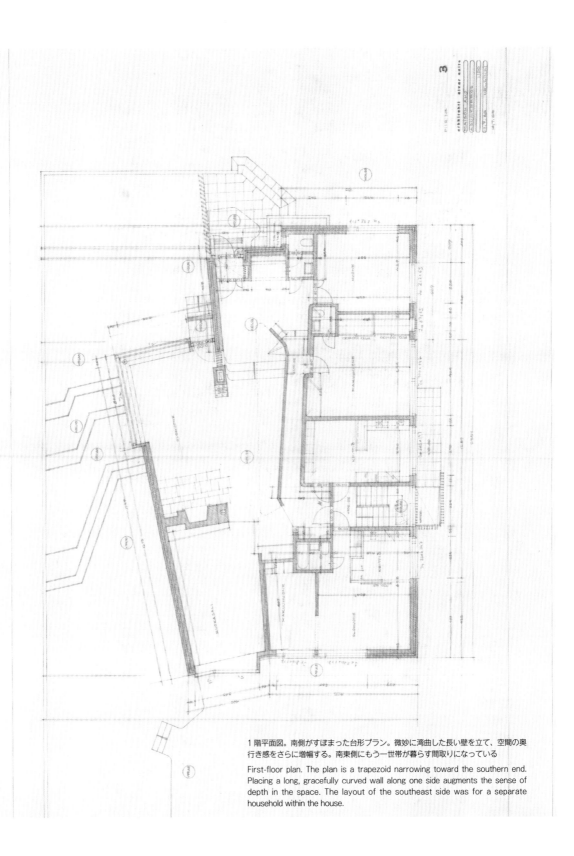

1階平面図。南側がすほまった台形プラン。微妙に湾曲した長い壁を立て、空間の奥行き感をさらに増幅する。南東側にもう一世帯が暮らす間取りになっている

First-floor plan. The plan is a trapezoid narrowing toward the southern end. Placing a long, gracefully curved wall along one side augments the sense of depth in the space. The layout of the southeast side was for a separate household within the house.

(右上) リビングルームのL形の出窓。北側の小さな中庭に向く

(右下) 東側、裏動線の出入り口。高窓格子から朝日を入れるのは、アールトの定石

(Top right) The L-shaped window in the living room faces a patio on the north side.

(Bottom right) East side, with the back entrance. Letting in light using a high window lattice was part of the Aalto design formula.

Maison Aho

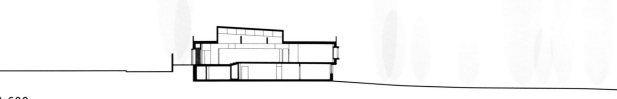

S 1:600

Ninety percent of Rovaniemi, located at 66 degrees latitude at the threshold of the Finnish province of Lapland near the Arctic Circle, was burned to the ground by the German army during World War II. Soon after the war Aalto created a reconstruction plan, and, while a number of years passed, his designs for community housing and commercial buildings were realized beginning in the latter part of the 1950s. From 1961 he supervised construction of a city library (1961–68), town hall (1963–66, built 1985–87), and theater (1969–76).

Commissions to build a commercial building and multi-unit housing in central areas of the town by Aarne Aho, a car dealer in Rovaniemi also serving as city council member, also date from this period in the late 1950s when Aalto's connections with the town grew close. This house was commissioned in 1964 and completed in the following year.

The site is part of a subdivided housing development and slopes southeast with the highest point on the front entrance side at the street. The southwest side at the time the house was completed and also today is a park. The horizontal lines of the long red-brick exterior wall and the stair-stepped sections of the brick fence make a striking sight from the park. Aalto originally planned to finish the wall with limewashing, but the client questioned its durability in local weather conditions, so it was left red-brick. The temperature in Rovaniemi goes down to as low as minus 20 degrees Celsius in the coldest part of winter, with the highest temperatures during the summer about 20 degrees, and half the year is harsh, snowy weather. The exterior walls of the house, as drawn in a sectional drawing, consist of an innermost 18-centimeter concrete wall, 10 centimeters of air insulation space, and a brick outer layer.

The plan is in a trapezoidal shape narrowing toward the back, southeast side. Looking into the house from the front entrance, we note the long, narrow skylight that stretches the length of the space beyond, casting soft natural light over a long, slightly curving wall along the left side. The highlight of the Aho house is the view from this position. The tapering plan accentuates the effect of a long perspective continuing 20 meters through the dining room at the far end and out through the windows, and the effect is further enhanced by the white wall on the left and the fireplace at the right. Behind the wall is a narrow corridor along which the bedrooms and other private spaces of the house are situated. This wall served as a gallery for

ロヴァニエミの行政・文化センター
Rovaniemi administrative and cultural center (1961–87).

北極圏に近いラップランドの玄関、北緯66度に位置するロヴァニエミは、第二次世界大戦中に町の90%をドイツ軍に焼き払われた。戦後、すぐにアールトはこの町の復興計画を立案した。時間を経て、50年代後半からアールトが設計した共同住宅や商業ビルの開発が実現していき、1961年からは、図書館（1961−68）、市役所（1963−66、建設1985−87）、劇場（1969−76）からなる計画が進められていった。ロヴァニエミの自動車販売業者で市会議員を務めていたアールネ・アホから、市の中心地に建てる商業ビルや集合住宅を依頼されたのも50年代後半からのことだった。この住宅は1964年に依頼され、翌年に竣工している。

　敷地は区画された住宅地のなか、玄関側が高くなった南東斜面で、南西側の隣地は竣工当時も今も公園となっている。そこから見ると、長く伸びる赤レンガの外壁の水平線と、傾斜に合わせて段上になったレンガ塀が印象的だ。アールトは最初、外壁の仕上げに白の石灰塗りを望んだが、施主は耐候性に疑問をもち、赤レンガ壁になったという。ロヴァニエミは最低気温が−20℃、最高気温が20℃ほどで、1年の半分は降雪のある気候である。断面図によれば、外壁には厚み18cmのコンクリート壁に10cmの空気層を設け、その外側にレンガを積んで二重壁にしている。

　プランは南東に向かってすぼまった台形になっている。室内に入ると、眼前には微妙に湾曲した長い壁が伸び、その壁は細長いスカイライトからの柔らかな自然光で照らされている。この地点からの眺めはアホ邸のハイライトである。奥にすぼまった台形プランのため、見え方にパースペクティブがつき、いちばん奥のダイニングルームの窓まで視線は一気に20m伸びて外へ抜けていく。長い壁の裏は細い廊下になっており、ベッドルームなどの個室が面する。施主は熱心なアートコレクターで、この壁の表の面はいわばギャラリーウォールとして機能し、当時は多くの絵がここに掛けられていた。壁上のスカイライトからは、朝には東から光が差す。強い反射光があたるのは、春から秋にかけては午前中、夏は早朝である。

　リビングルームは、北西にあるパティオへ向けてL形のガラス窓で大きく開いている。塀で囲まれたこの庭は、外からの視線を遮断したプライベート空間である。アールトが北庭を取るのは珍しい。光の質量が変化に富んだ、家の奥の南側にリビングと庭をもっていかずに、玄関からすぐ脇に配置したのは何か理由があったのだろう。平面図を見ると、当初、この家は二世帯住宅になっており、ダイニングルームの隣の南東側にもう一世帯用の空間を取る必要があったようだ。もしこの条件がなければ、まったく別のプランができていたのではないだろうか。現在は所有が変わり、間取りは変更されている。

玄関側
Front facade.

正面玄関
Front entrance.

the owner, an enthusiastic collector of art, and many paintings hung on this wall when the Aho family lived here. The skylight illuminates this private gallery with the eastern sun in the morning, and with strong reflected light in the early mornings of summer and during the morning hours from spring to fall.

The living room is opened wide through an L-shaped window facing the patio on the northwest. Enclosed by the wall encircling the property, the courtyard is a private space sheltered from sight. This is a rare example of a garden by Aalto positioned on the north side. The reason Aalto placed the courtyard and the living room alongside the entrance way rather than on the southern side of the house, where there would have been ample and varied light, was probably that at the time the house was built, it was meant to include two households. He added the necessary rooms for the other household on the southeast side next to the dining room. If that situation had not prevailed, the plan would probably have been quite different. Ownership has since changed hands and some parts of the room layout have been changed from the original plan.

パティオに面するL形の窓
L-shaped window facing the patio.

エンソ・グッツァイト社宅
Enso-Gutzeit Engineers' & Managers' Houses
Summa, Finland (1958－1964)

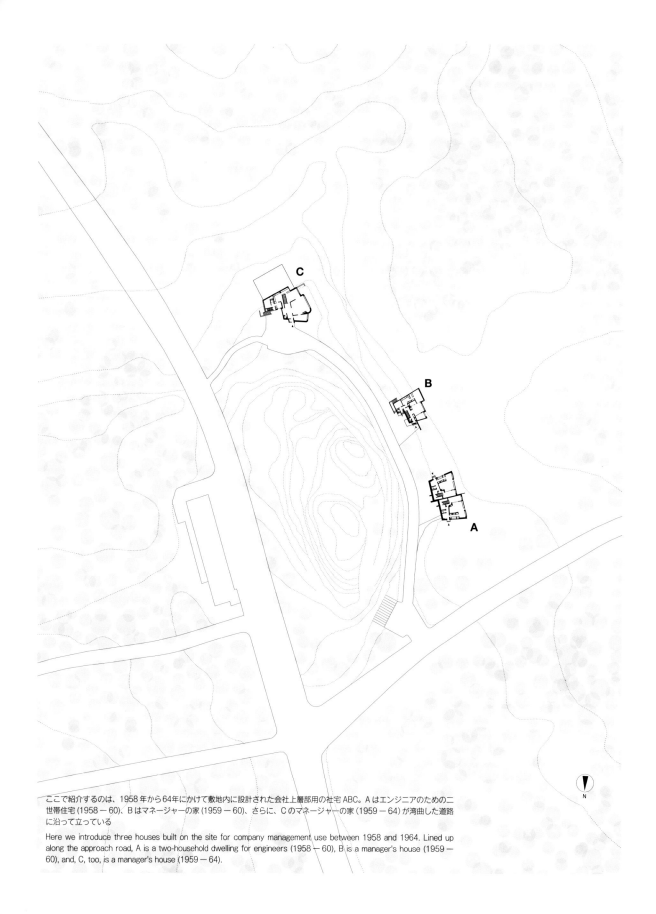

ここで紹介するのは、1958年から64年にかけて敷地内に設計された会社上層部用の社宅ABC。Aはエンジニアのための二世帯住宅(1958－60)、Bはマネージャーの家(1959－60)、さらに、Cのマネージャーの家(1959－64)が湾曲した道路に沿って立っている

Here we introduce three houses built on the site for company management use between 1958 and 1964. Lined up along the approach road, A is a two-household dwelling for engineers (1958 － 60), B is a manager's house (1959 － 60), and, C, too, is a manager's house (1959 － 64).

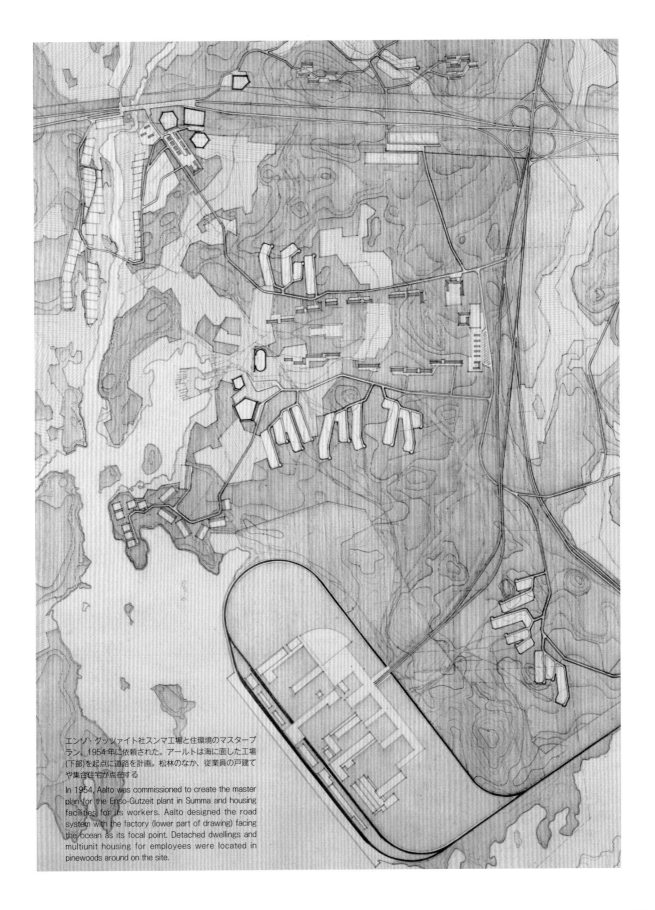

エンゾ・グッツァイト社スンマ工場と住環境のマスタープラン。1954年に依頼された。アールトは海に面した工場（下部）を起点に道路を計画。松林のなか、従業員の戸建てや集合住宅が点在する

In 1954, Aalto was commissioned to create the master plan for the Enso-Gutzeit plant in Summa and housing facilities for its workers. Aalto designed the road system with the factory (lower part of drawing) facing the ocean as its focal point. Detached dwellings and multiunit housing for employees were located in pinewoods around on the site.

右側の岩と同じ輪郭をした建築の形
Note how the contours of the great rock resonate with the roofline of the houses.

マネージャーの家 C の庭側
Manager's house C from the garden side.

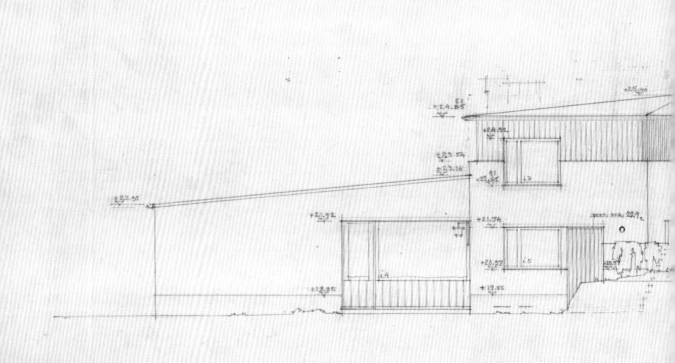

東から見たマネージャーの家C。斜面に立ち、上階にある玄関側は道路付けで、下階の東側半分は地面と接する。壁と屋根の間に横長の格子窓を挟み、軽快にまとめたデザイン

Manager's house C seen from east side. Built on a slope, the upper floor faces the road on the front entrance side. The east-side half of the lower floor hugs the ground. The high window lattice between wall and roof gives a light touch to the design.

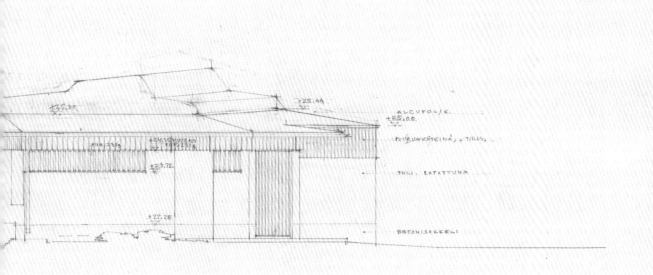

ALUSTAVA

ENSO-GUTZEIT OY,
SUMMAN TEHTAAT, JOHTAJAN ASUNTO I
JULKISIVU ITÄÄN   1/50   PIIR, N:o 206
H:KI   30. 4. -59   ALVAR AALTO, ARKKITEHTI
       27. 5. -59

玄関扉を開けると、五つの部屋へ通じる廊下に出る。ここは手のひらの中央にいるような地点で、右手に書斎とリビングルーム、正面奥にダイニング、左はキッチンへ通じる廊下。下階にはベッドルームがある

The front entrance door opens on a corridor leading to five rooms. On the right are the study and living room. Straight ahead in the back is the dining room, and to the left the hall leading to the kitchen. The bedrooms are on the lower floor down the stairs. This spot is like the center of the palm of a hand.

午後の光。床に反射した光が天井へ拡散する
Afternoon light. Light reflected off the floor shines against the ceiling.

林の景をリズミカルに切りとる窓。奥には書斎がある
The rhythmical lines of the windows capture the landscape of the woods.

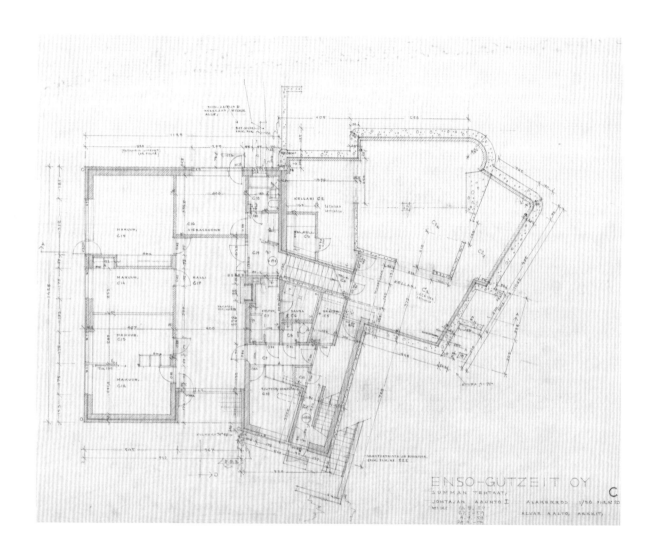

下階平面図。1959年9月24日。この家は典型的なフィンガーフォームのプランで、プライベートエリア（下階）とパブリックエリア（上階）に分け、それぞれを東と西の異なる方位へ向けている。ベッドルームは南東向きで朝日がふんだんに入射する。中央にサウナがある

Lower floor plan, dated September 24, 1959. This design displays Aalto's typical "finger form"; it divides the private areas (lower floor) from the public areas (upper floor) facing opposite directions, the former to the east and the latter to the west. The bedrooms face southeast, and are flooded with sunshine in the morning. The sauna is in the center of the house.

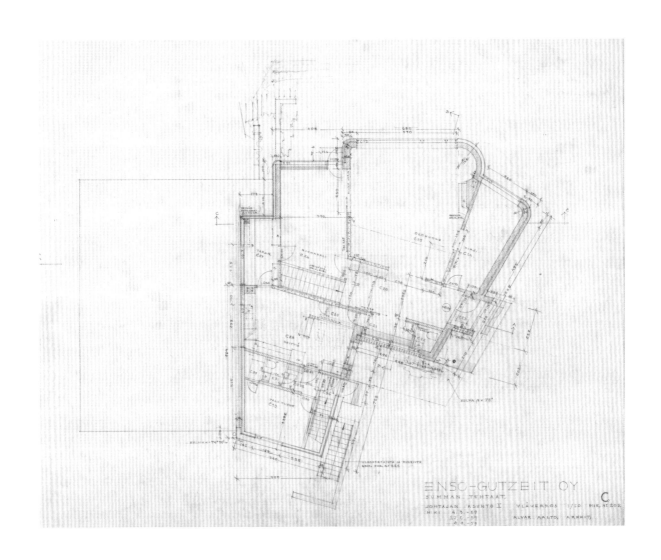

上階平面図。1959年9月4日。右から書斎、リビングルーム、ダイニングルームの配置で、すべて南西に大きく開いている。下階は朝の光、上階は午後からの光を楽しむ空間。階段が2カ所にあり、裏動線となる東側(下部)の階段はメイド室の脇につく

Upper floor plan. The layout shows the study, living room, and dining room, all opened wide to the southwest. The lower floor contains the spaces for enjoying the light of morning and the upper floor the light of afternoon. There are two flights of stairs and the east-side stairs (lower part) that provide the behind-the-scenes lines of movement pass by the maid's quarters.

社宅AとBを見る。岩に呼応した屋根の形態
View of the A and B houses. The shapes of their roofs echo the lines of the great rock beyond.

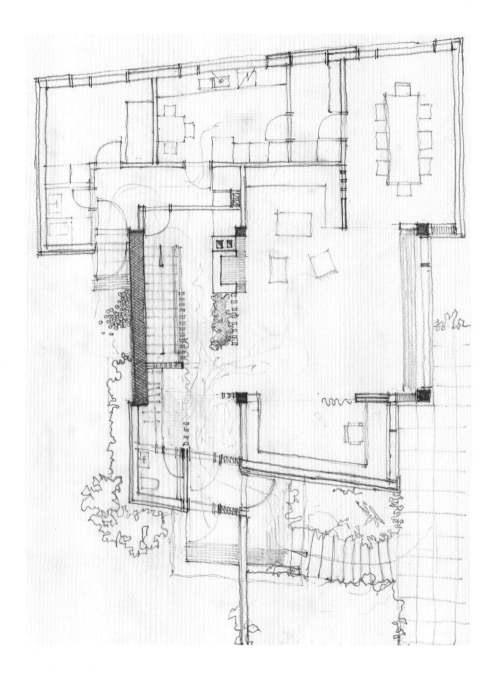

(上) 社宅 B のスケッチプラン(上階)。現在ゲストハウスとなっているが、当初のまま使われている。プランの基本形は3軒とも同じで、西の林へ向けて扇形に開き、扇の要にあたる部分に階段を取る。薄い鉛筆の線で人の動きがスタディされている
(右上) 林の景色へ開いたリビングルーム
(右下) 格子の奥は階段。下階にはベッドルームがある

(Above) Sketch plan of manager's house B (upper floor). Now mainly a guest house, it continues to be used as it was originally built. The basic shape of the plan is the same for all three houses, fanning out toward the woods on the west, with stairwells at the pivot of the fan. Faint pencil lines show the architect's study of lines of movement within the house.
(Top right) The living room windows open out on the wooded landscape.
(Bottom right) Beyond the lattice are the stairs. The bedrooms are on the lower level.

3軒のうち最初に建てられた二世帯住宅 A。西の林側から見る

Seen from the woods to the west, the company house A for two-households was the first of the three to be built.

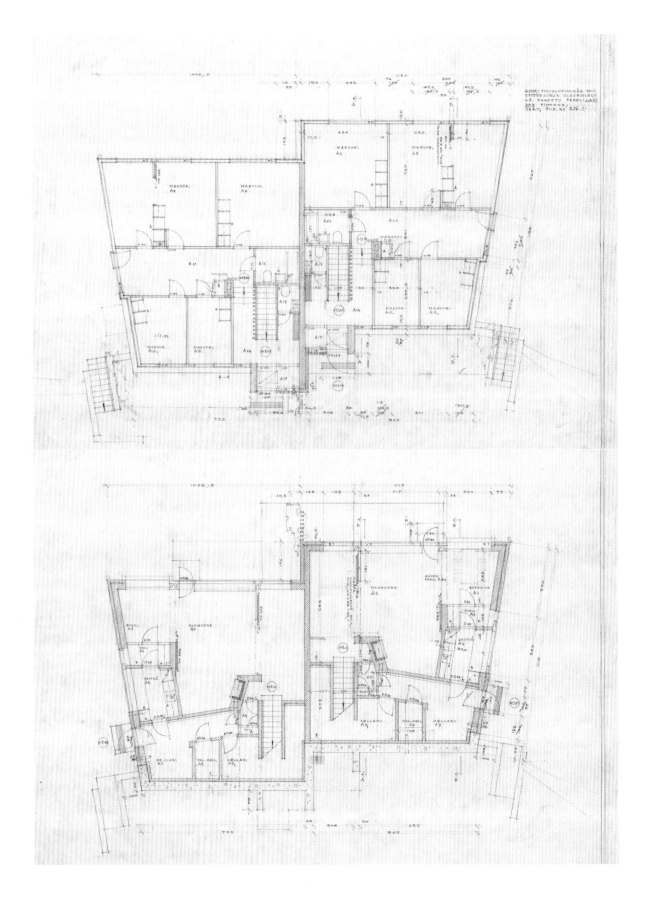

304

（左）二世帯住宅Ａの平面図。上階に玄関があるのは３軒共通だが、この家は下階にリビングやダイニングがあり（下図）、上階に寝室がある（上図）
（右上）リビングからダイニングへ。ひとつながりの空間
（右下）コンパクトで機能的なキッチン

(Left) Plans of the company house A for two-households. All three houses have their front entrances on the upper floor, but this house has the living and dining rooms on the lower floor (bottom), with the bedrooms on the upper floor (top).
(Top right) View from the living room toward the dining room.
(Bottom right) The kitchen is compact and functional.

Enso-Gutzeit Engineers' & Managers' Houses

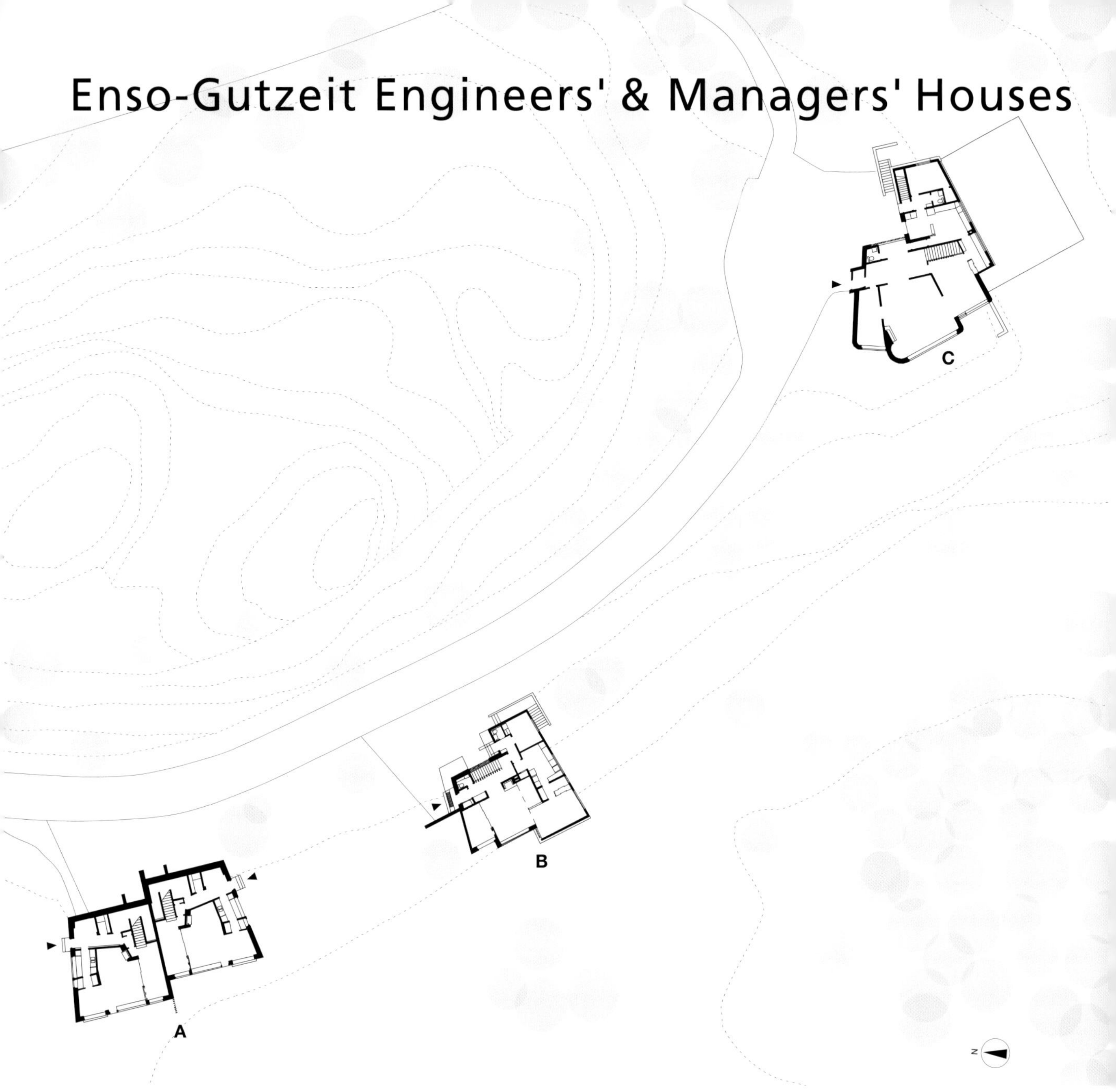

C

B

A

N

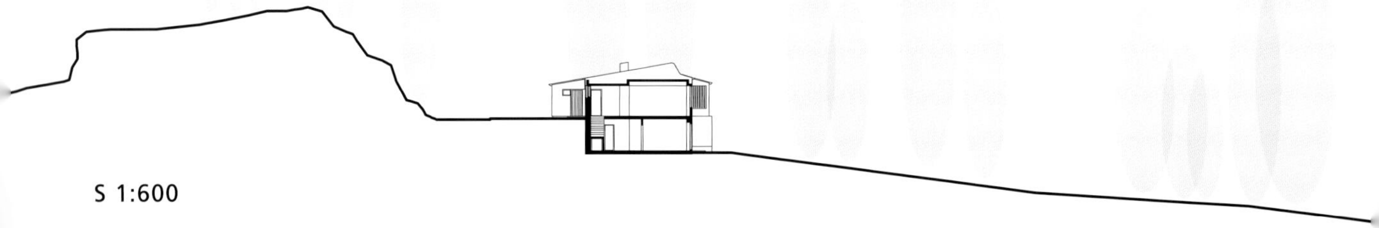

S 1:600

Alvar Aalto's links with the business world were close. The architect's career, beginning before World War II, was inextricably connected especially to paper manufacturing, one of Finland's major industries. He remained involved for a long period in designing the master plans for towns centering on the factories of the Toppila Pulp Mill (1930–33; Oulu), Sunila Pulp Mill (1936–54; Kotka), and Tampella (1937–54; Inkeroinen) and in the environmental development planning including everything from large-scale factory facilities to homes for employees.

His work for Enso-Gutzeit (now Stora Enso) also goes back to 1932, when the as-yet nameless architect participated in a competition for the company's weekend villa. From soon after the war and into the 1950s, Aalto built many single dwellings and multi-unit housing projects for the company using his "AA system" for the standardized, low-cost housing plan the company provided its workers. In 1954, in the town of Summa on the coast about 130 kilometers east of Helsinki, the company planned to build a large-scale paper-making factory and put Aalto in charge of its master plan. He was asked to design not just the factory, but a whole community with employee housing, schools, sports facilities, and shops. The three houses included here are part of the works completed for the company on its vast site.

Of particular interest regarding these houses is Aalto's reading of the setting. Visiting the site after receiving the commission, he found it to be completely undeveloped, open country. Finland is not mountainous and relatively flat and most of the land is granite-based covered with a thin layer of soil, but the site has a rise of about 10 meters and a huge two-humped granite outcrop, which seems to have offered valuable design hints to the architect. Making the most of the natural landscape, the road curves around this outcrop and the houses are positioned along the line of the road. The west side of the road is a slope covered with red-pine forest. Of the three houses, the first to be designed was the northernmost two-household dwelling (1958–60; now called the VIP House) and was meant for company engineers and their families. The next was the Manager's House to the south (1959–60; now the Guest House), and the third is the other Manager's House, yet further south (1959–64). The third occupies the largest area and is the house that continues to be used by the factory manager and his family.

アールトと企業家とのつながりは深い。とくに、フィンランドの根幹産業である製紙業とこの建築家のキャリアとは切っても切れない関係にある。それは戦前からはじまる。トッピラ・パルプ工場（1930−33、オウル）、スニラ・パルプ工場（1936−54、コトカ）やタンペラ社（1937−54、インケロイネン）の工場を中心とした町のマスタープランなど、大規模な工場施設からそこで働く人々の住居を含めた環境整備計画まで、アールトは長期にわたって関与している。

エンソ・グッツァイト社（現ストラ・エンソ社）とのつきあいも、まだアールトが無名だった1932年の週末別荘のコンペからはじまっている。戦後すぐから50年代にかけては、アールトが「AAシステム」と名づけた、規格化したローコストのハウジングプランが同社の労働者向け住居に採用され、数多くの一戸建て、集合住宅が建てられた。1954年には、ヘルシンキから海岸沿いに130kmほど東へ行った町スンマに、同社は大規模な製紙工場を建てる計画を立てるが、このときアールトはマスタープランをまかされる。そこは工場のみならず、雇用者の住宅、学校、スポーツ施設、商店などを組みこんだ一大コミュニティとして構想された。この三つの社宅もその一部で、同社の広大な敷地内にある。

この一連の社宅で面白いのは、アールトの土地の読みである。依頼されて敷地を見に行ったとき周囲は整備されておらず、原野に近い状態だった。フィンランドは山がなく、国土のほとんどが平地で、花崗岩板の上にわずかな土がかぶさっている場所がほとんどであるが、この敷地には10mほど盛りあがった、フタコブラクダのような形をした巨岩がある。これは建築家にとっては、デザインの足がかりをつかむ貴重な「山」だったはずである。自然の景観を生かして、道路はその岩山を取り囲むようにしてゆるやかに湾曲をつけて設置され、3軒の家がその道路ラインに沿って配置されている。道路の西側は、赤松林の広がる下り斜面である。3軒の住宅のうち、最初に設計されたのがいちばん北側に位置する二世帯住宅（1958−60、現VIPハウス）で、これは工場の技師とその家族用の住まいである。つぎに、その南側に工場長の住宅が設計され（1959−60、現ゲストハウス）、さらに南寄りにもう1軒、工場長の家が設計されている（1959−64）。これがいちばん大きな面積があり、現在も工場長の一家が住居として使っている。

まず、3軒に共通するのは、ぎざぎざに隆起をつけた屋根のシルエットである。アールトは、道路を挟んで横たわるフタコブラクダの岩の形に呼応するようにして、これらの屋根のシルエットを決めている。3軒とも斜面に建てられており、仕上げも同じで、林につながる下階は石灰塗りのレンガ、道路につながる上階は黒く塗った縦の羽目板張りで、上下が黒と白のコンビである。西側の

松林側から見た社宅B
Garden facade of the house B.

The feature shared by all three houses is the zigzagging contour of the roof silhouettes. Aalto designed the silhouettes of the three houses to resonate with the two-humped shape of the outcropping across the road. All three are built on a slope in the same style, a combination of black and white, the lower floor opening out on the woods of limewashed brick and the upper floor facing the road covered with black-painted vertical siding. The three also share plans that fan out to the west toward the woods with the living rooms and dining rooms in the open parts and large windows that incorporate the pine-forest vista into the dwelling. The entrances of all three houses are located on the upper floor, opening out on the road.

None of these houses are order-made dwellings designed for specific clients with whom the architect worked face-to-face. They were designs conceived on the basis of information obtained about family composition, desired number of rooms, area, and available funds. Aalto was dedicated in the development of housing plans that could be quickly and easily built at low cost to create better living environments for people who had lost their homes during and after the war and for factory workers. He developed standard plans, but as a policy he was opposed to the adoption of uniform housing. He aimed to design plans consisting of a basic dwelling core with elements that could be adapted to the environment of the site, family composition, household income, and other variations in individual conditions.

The social position of the residents of these three houses was high, so they probably cannot be considered to fall in the line of standard-style dwellings he worked on after the war, but in some respects they are a developed form of such dwellings. Designed within a certain conceptual framework, they are houses that assure a quality and comfortable lifestyle to anyone who might move into them. It is achievement that might seem easy but is in fact quite difficult. In general, in most cases it is much easier for an architect to deal with details when a client generates specific conditions and requests. Since Aalto was devoted to developing housing according to various standard plans for some time earlier, he must have accumulated many ideas about lifestyle simulation and plan variation, so these company housing designs would have been further applications of those ideas.

Of the three houses, the largest manager's house displays a design combining Aalto's

社宅Bのリビングルーム
Living room of the house B.

赤松林に向かって扇状に開くプランにしているのも共通項で、開いた部分にはリビングルームとダイニングルームがあり、大きな窓を開けて林の景観が室内に取りこまれている。玄関は、どの住宅も道路付けで上階に位置する。

この3軒は、「顔の見える」特定の施主のために設計されたオーダーメイドの住宅ではない。家族構成、相応する個室数、面積、経済に見合った暮らし方などをあくまで想定して設計された社宅である。アールトは戦中戦後、家を失った人々や労働者の生活環境整備のため、ローコストで素早く容易に建てられる住宅プランの開発に心血を注いだ。だが、規格化はしても「画一化」はしないのがアールトのポリシーだった。彼は最小限住宅を母体に、敷地環境や家族構成、経済的余裕など、個別の状況や変化に対応できる余地をもつプランづくりを目指した。この3軒の社宅は、住み手の社会的地位も高く、アールトが戦後に取りくんだ一連の規格化住宅の流れには入らないだろうが、ある側面ではその発展形ともいえる。想定された枠組のなかで、誰が移ってきて住んでも質の高い快適な暮らしを実現できる家となっているのである。これは簡単なようでいて、じつは難しい。概して建築家にとっては、具体的な条件やリクエストがクライアントから出された方が、細やかな対応ができる場合が多いからである。住宅の規格化に徹底して取りくんだ時期があったからこそ、アールトの頭のなかには、住み方のシミュレーションやプランのヴァリエーションが蓄積されていたのだろう。このような社宅のデザインは、いわばその応用編だったはずである。

なかでもいちばん大きな工場長の家は、アールトの建築ヴォキャブラリーの、オーダーメイドとレディメードを掛けあわせたようなデザインになっている。まさしくオーダーメイド的なアプローチでのぞんだヴィラ・マイレアやメゾン・カレのような強い個性はないものの、この家はほかの2軒の社宅とは別格である。それを可能にしたのは、玄関を入った地点で目に入るリビングルームの木の天井と、その下の大きな窓のリズミカルなデザインである。

竣工から半世紀を経ても、これらの社宅は美しくメンテナンスされて今も使われている。フレキシブルなプランと動線計画、適切な面積配分、光と風の入れ方、シンプルなディテールなど、アールトの提案がいかに優れていたかをこのことは証明している。

社宅C・リビングルームの窓
Living room windows of the house C.

vocabulary of both made-to-order and ready-made dwellings. Although it does not have the distinctive look that he achieved in such made-to-order approaches as adopted for the Villa Mairea and Maison Carré, this house is clearly of a different class from the other two. That distinction is afforded by the pine wood ceiling in the living room and the large windows beneath it with their rhythmically sized panes, visible upon entering the entrance.

Half a century since they were completed, these dwellings are still in use and beautifully maintained as company housing. They are eloquent examples of the quality of Aalto's ideas on flexible planning, attention to lines of movement, distribution of space, allowances for light and ventilation, simple details, and other aspects of design.

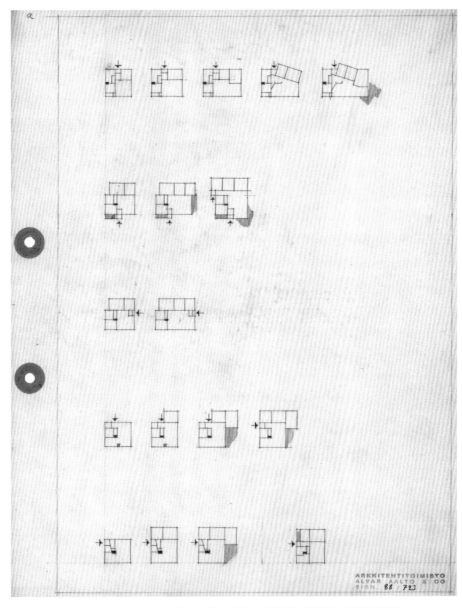

戦前から戦後にかけて、アールトはローコストでプレファブ化した住宅のタイプデザインを開発した。図はその展開例
From before World War II and afterwards, Aalto developed various standardized house designs that could be prefabricated and built at low cost. The drawing shows the various configurations possible with the AA-System house plan.

ヴィラ・タンメカン

Villa Tammekkann

Tartu, Estonia (1932－1933)

南に面する庭側。1階の連窓のなかはリビング、左側のテラスはダイニングとつながる

Side facing garden on the south. Beyond the strip windows is the living room; to the left is the dining room linked to the terrace.

東側を見る。2階のベッドルームについた小さなバルコニー。1階奥にはパーゴラをつけたテラスが見える。太陽が燦々と降り注ぐ開放的なバルコニーは、「モダンハウス」に不可欠の要素だった

View of the east side. Note the small balcony of the second-floor bedroom. Also visible is the ground-floor terrace with pergola at the back. The open balcony filled with sunshine was one of the indispensable elements of the "modern house."

バウハウスのヴォキャブラリーで構成された北側ファサード。パイミオのサナトリウム竣工後すぐに建てられた。1930年代に分譲された住宅地に立つ。当時エストニアでは、陸屋根はまだ珍しかった

The north facade composition is faithful to the Bauhaus vocabulary. Built soon after completion of the Paimio Sanatorium, it is located in a residential district opened up in the 1930s. Flat roofs were a still novelty in Estonia at this time.

(左) リビングルーム。暖炉の煙突は庭への視界を遮断しないように、左側の壁内に横に通している。大きな扉は一本引きで、奥には書斎がある
(上) リビングルームとつながるダイニングルーム

(Left) Living room. The chimney for the fireplace is built into the wall on the left, passing horizontally in order not to interrupt the view of the garden. The large sliding door opens on the study at the other end of the room.
(Above) The dining room linked to the living room.

（左上）ダイニングルームの二重サッシの窓と扉。70cmほど間隙を空け、小さな風除け室として機能。断熱しつつ、少しでも多くの光を採りいれようとしている

（右上）リビングルームの連窓。部屋の奥行きが浅いため、右の矩形図が示すようにサッシをぎりぎりまで外側へ設置し、内部と外部との一体感をつくりだそうとしている

（下）半地階にあるサウナ。2000年の改修時、ビジター用に設けられた

(Top left) The double-sash window and door of the dining room. The sashes are about 70 centimeters apart, creating a small wind-buffer chamber. While helping to insulate the house, it allows for as much sunshine to enter as possible.

(Top right) Strip windows in the living room. The depth of the room is limited, so, as indicated by the sectional detail drawings on the right page, the windows are set as close to the outside as possible, an effect that further accentuates the closeness of inside and outside.

(Bottom) The sauna was added for visitors when the house was renovated in 2000.

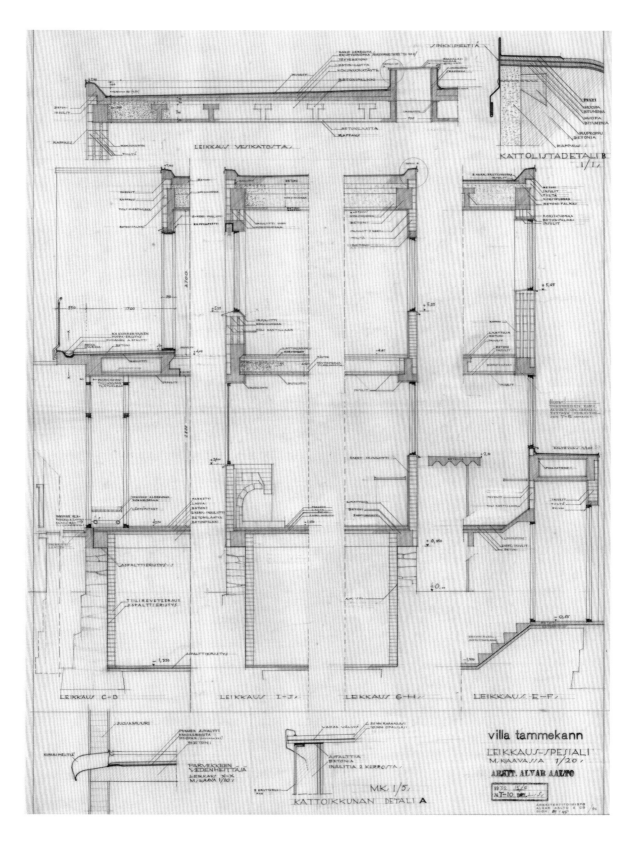

villa tammekann

LEIKKAUS–SPESIALI
M. KAAVASSA 1/20

ARKT. ALVAR AALTO

矩形詳細図。屋根・壁とも空気層を挟んだ二重壁にし、外気を遮る設計。断熱性能を高めるためのディテールが興味深い

Sectional detail drawings. Both walls and roof are double-layered with airspace between to shut out the cold. The details of the design worked out to enhance heat-retaining functions are of great interest.

Villa Tammekkann

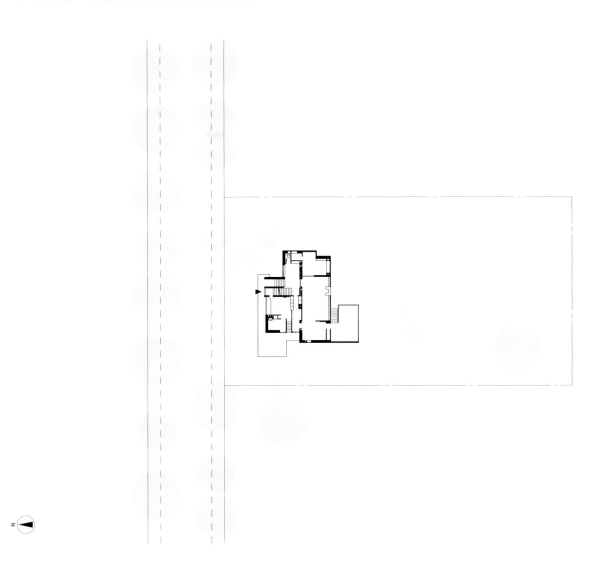

The Villa Tammekann is the private home that most markedly shows the influence of functionalism on Aalto, who did the design at the age of 34. The house is located in Tartu, Estonia, south of Finland across the Baltic Sea, an old university town about 190 kilometers southeast of the capital of Tallinn.

Estonian geographer August Tammekann became acquainted with Aalto through J. G. Granö, who was a professor of geography and rector of Finland's University of Turku. Emerging as an up-and-coming architect, Aalto left his home in Jyväskylä in 1927, opened an office in the southwestern port city of Turku, and participated for the first time in the second Congrès Internationaux d'Architecture Moderne (CIAM) at Frankfurt in 1929. There he got to know Walter Gropius, Le Corbusier, and Sigfried Giedion, and absorbed their ideas through visits to houses built in the functionalist style they advocated. Aalto was close to completion of the work on the Paimio Tuberculosis Sanatorium that was to become the most famous of his works, and his future seemed assured. Finland, however, had suffered the full impact of the Great Depression in October 1929, so once the Sanatorium was completed, Aalto would have had almost no specific project left on his drawing board.

The commission from the Tammekanns was a godsend and the couple were ideal clients for Aalto. They were of the same generation as he and keenly interested in the new architectural trends then emerging in Europe. It was they who submitted the request for a modern, practical, functionalist-style house with a flat roof, open-style balcony and terrace, and equipped with a modern kitchen.

The time was ripe for the new architecture, for which Estonia and Finland then shared a particular receptiveness. Finland in 1917 and Estonia in 1918 had become independent from Soviet Russia and both newborn nations were in the throes of innovation and change. As functionalist architecture gained momentum in the 1920s, both countries actively embraced the new style as a symbol of independence, freedom, and the advent of a new era. Prior to this house—as early as the late 1920s—functionalist-style flat-roof houses were being built by local architects in Estonia, but in a country of heavy snows, the suitability of the flat roof to the climate was the stuff of vigorous debate.

パイミオのサナトリウム
Paimio Tuberculosis Sanatorium (1929–32).

パイミオのサナトリウム、日光浴のためのバルコニー
Solarium level of the Paimio Sanatorium.

ヴィラ・タンメカンはアールトが34歳のときの作品で、機能主義（ファンクショナリズム）の影響をもっとも色濃く残した個人住宅である。

　この家はバルト海を挟んでフィンランドの南向かい、エストニアのタルトゥにある。首都のタリンから190kmほど南東に位置する古い大学町である。エストニア人で地理学者のアウグスト・タンメカンとアールトは、フィンランドのトゥルク大学の地理学教授で学長のJ. G. グラーノを通して知りあう。故郷のユヴァスキラを1927年に離れ、南西部の港湾都市トゥルクに事務所を構えた新進気鋭の建築家アールトは、1929年にはフランクフルトで開催された第2回CIAM（近代建築国際会議）に初めて参加し、主催者であるグロピウスやル・コルビュジエ、ギーディオンたちと親交を深め、彼らの提唱する機能主義スタイルの住宅を見てまわり、吸収していた。アールトは、のちに彼の記念碑的作品となるパイミオのサナトリウムの完成を間近に控え、将来は順風満帆に見えた。ところが、1929年10月に起こった世界大恐慌でフィンランドも深刻な不景気に見舞われ、サナトリウムが竣工すれば、アールトの製図台に具体的なプロジェクトはほとんどなかったという。

　そんな折、タンメカン夫妻からの依頼は願ってもないタイミングだったにちがいない。しかも、アールトにとっては理想的なクライアントだった。同世代だった彼らは、ヨーロッパで起こりつつあった新しい建築の潮流に関心を寄せていた。陸屋根、開放的なバルコニーとテラス、近代的なキッチンを備えた現代的で実用的な機能主義スタイルの家がほしい。そんな要望を最初に出したのは、夫妻の方だったという。

　これには時代背景もある。この頃のエストニアとフィンランドは、新しい建築を受けいれる素地に共通点があった。フィンランドは1917年、エストニアは1918年にロシアから独立し、新生した両国には刷新の空気がみなぎっていた。1920年代から機能主義の潮流が起きると、両国ではこの新しいスタイルが独立と自由、新時代の幕開けの象徴として受けいれられようとしていた。エストニアではこの住宅に先行して、早くも1920年代末から陸屋根の機能主義スタイルの家が地元の建築家によって建てられはじめた。雪の多いこの国で、平らな屋根が風土に適しているのかどうか、当時論争が巻き起こったという。

　ヴィラ・タンメカンの外観は、白壁、キャノピー、連窓、テラス、ガレージ、パーゴラなど、アールトの先達たちが唱えた機能主義のヴォキャブラリーに沿ってデザインされている。この作品のなかでアールトの独自性が感じられるのは、むしろ内部空間である。1926年に書いたエッセイ *From Doorstep to Living Room*（玄関からリビングルームまで）[11] で、内部と外部空間をつなげ、

道路側ファサード
Street facade.

The Villa Tammekann exterior, with its white walls, canopy, strip windows, terrace, garage, and pergola, is designed using the functionalist vocabulary of earlier advocates. In this work, Aalto's personal style is more evident in the interior. Early in his career, as argued in his 1926 essay, "*From Doorstep to Living Room*,"[11] Aalto sought to link inside and outside spaces and to open up houses to the landscape outside, and he held to this idea to the end of his life. The Villa Tammekann living room, too, features large strip windows that open wide on the garden beyond. The fireplace, seats arranged before it, is situated under the windows as a kind of pivot linking inside and outside. In order to prevent anything from ruining the view, it should be noted, the fireplace's chimney has been routed horizontally through the adjacent waist-high wall on the left side. This must make it more difficult to start a fire in the fireplace, but it clearly demonstrates how firmly Aalto was determined to link the inside and outside.

Perhaps the most appealing feature of this house is the smooth continuity of the spaces—from entrance hall to living room, from living room either to dining room or study. With sliding doors and other devices, he uses flexible means of dividing the space and unites the whole into a single space. Two years after doing this house, Aalto designed his own home in the suburbs of Helsinki, and there, too, he uses a sliding door to allow for a flexible partition between the living room and his workplace. The concept of a single space centering on the living room was to become a characteristic of Aalto's houses, as eminently demonstrated in the Villa Mairea.

At the time the Villa Tammekann was originally built, a number of central features including the living room fireplace were not realized. Plagued by leaks, moreover, the flat roof was replaced in the 1950s with a gabled roof. In 1991, when Estonia regained its independence from the Soviet Union, ownership of the house was restored to the Tammekanns and in 1998, the University of Turku purchased the house and restored it faithfully according to Aalto's original plan.

リビングルーム
Living room.

ダイニングルーム
Dining room.

自然を室内に取りこむ重要性をアールトは早くも主張しているが、この考えは晩年まで一貫して変わらない。ヴィラ・タンメカンでも、リビングルームに連窓を設け、内部空間を庭へ大きく開いている。その窓下に暖炉を設置して庭と内部とを結ぶ要にし、暖炉を囲んで椅子を配置している。面白いのは、そのとき暖炉の煙突が庭への視界を台無しにしないよう、連窓の腰壁のなかへ水平に煙突を通すよう設計している点である。こうすると暖炉に火を起こすのはかなり難しくなるはずだが、内と外とのつながりを強く求めたアールトの明確な意図が表われている。

　この家のいちばんの魅力は、空間の滑らかな推移と連続感である。玄関ホールからリビングルーム、リビングからダイニングや書斎へと、空間の境界は引き戸などを使ってゆるやかに区切られ、全体がシングルスペースのようにまとめられている。この2年後にアールトはヘルシンキ郊外に自邸を設計するが、そこでもリビングと仕事場との境界を引き戸でフレキシブルに仕切れるようにしている。リビングを中心にしたシングルスペースのコンセプトは、以降、ヴィラ・マイレアを代表作にして、アールト住宅の特徴となっていく。

　ヴィラ・タンメカンは建設時、リビングの暖炉などいくつかの中心的なデザイン要素が実現しなかった。また、雨漏りに悩まされた陸屋根は、1950年代には寄せ棟に改造された。1991年、エストニアが旧ソ連からふたたび独立すると、家の所有権はタンメカン一族に返還され、98年にはトゥルク大学が買いあげて、アールトの原案に沿って忠実に修復されている。

1階平面図
First-floor plan.

2階平面図
Second-floor plan.

パイミオのサナトリウムを彷彿させる階段
Stairway, reminiscent of the stairs in the Paimio Sanatorium.

2階ベッドルーム
Bedroom on the second floor.

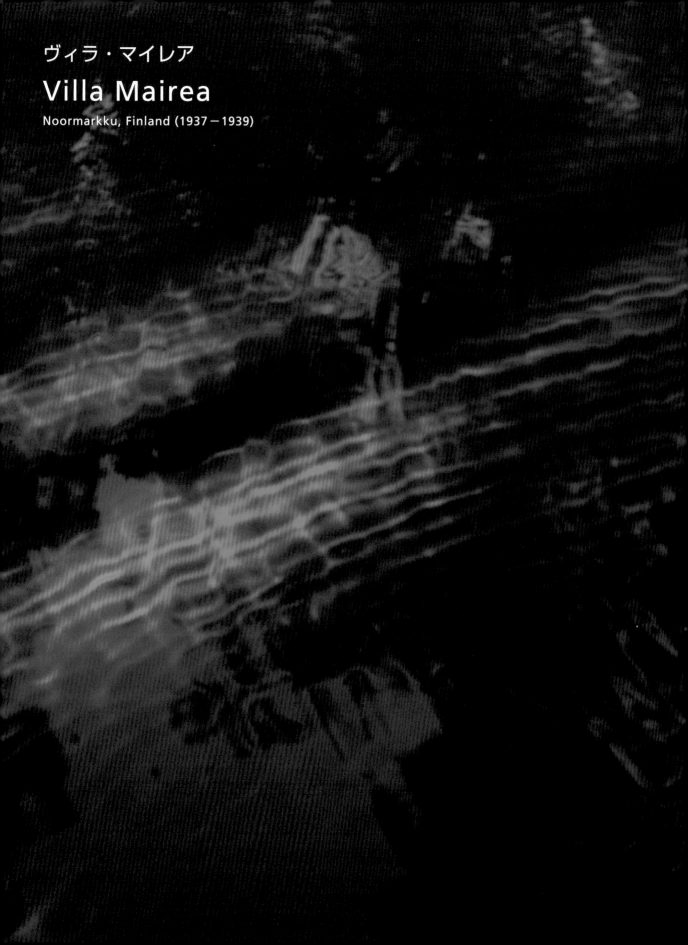

ヴィラ・マイレア
Villa Mairea
Noormarkku, Finland (1937 — 1939)

ノールマルク川がゆったりと流れる広大な敷地のなか、小丘の上に立つ
On a vast property through which the Noormarkku river winds, the villa stands on a small hill.

朝日を浴びる南東向きの玄関ファサード
Front facade, facing southeast, gets the morning sun.

玄関キャノピーの格子には細い丸太が使われており、周囲の林の景色と融けあう
The lattice of the entrance canopy is made of slender logs, echoing the textures of surrounding woods.

フリーフォームのキャノピーと丸太を組みあわせる。モダニズムのヴォキャブラリーと風土を喚起する素材との調和

The free-form canopy and rustic lattice create a pleasant harmony between the vocabulary of modernism and materials evoking the natural features of Finland.

玄関扉からキャノピー越しに松林を見る
Looking out to the pinewoods from inside the canopied entrance.

玄関ホール。曲面の白壁が奥の暖炉へと視線を導く
Entrance hall. The curving white wall guides the line of vision all the way back to the fireplace.

5月初め、夜9時頃の光。プールに反射した夕日がエントランスホールを照らす
About 9:00 p.m. in early May. Evening ray reflected off the pool comes into the entrance hall.

この家の最大の魅力は、階段を上がりつつ視界に入る眺めと空間の連続感
The great attraction of this house is the sense of continuity of the scene and spaces that unfold as one ascends the steps.

午後、西日を受けるサウナを室内から見る
The sauna hut in the afternoon sun, as seen from the living room.

床素材の切り替え、林立する柱が空間の奥行きを増幅する
A shift in flooring material and a group of columns enhance the sense of depth in the space.

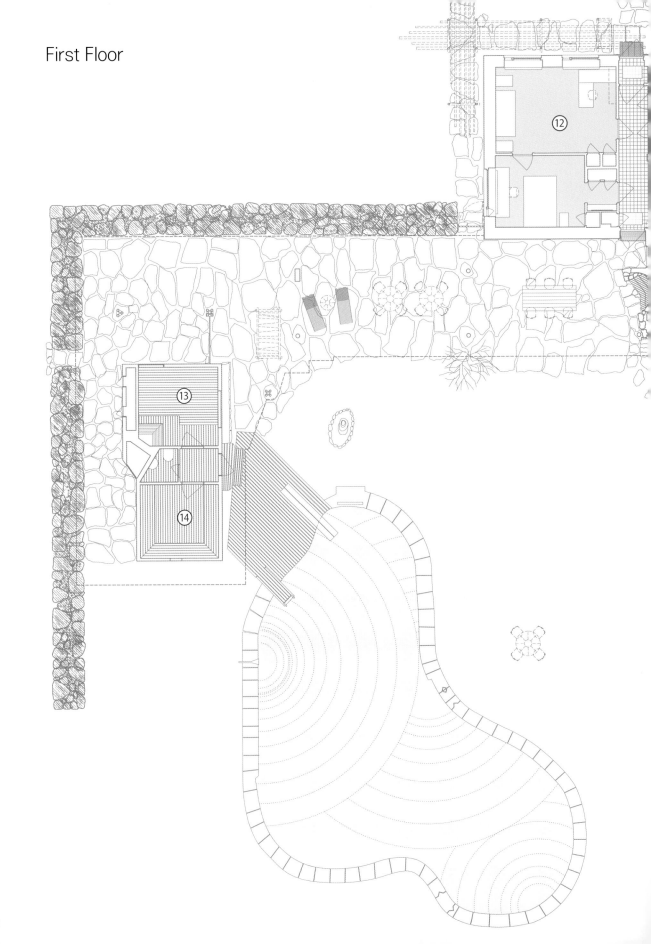

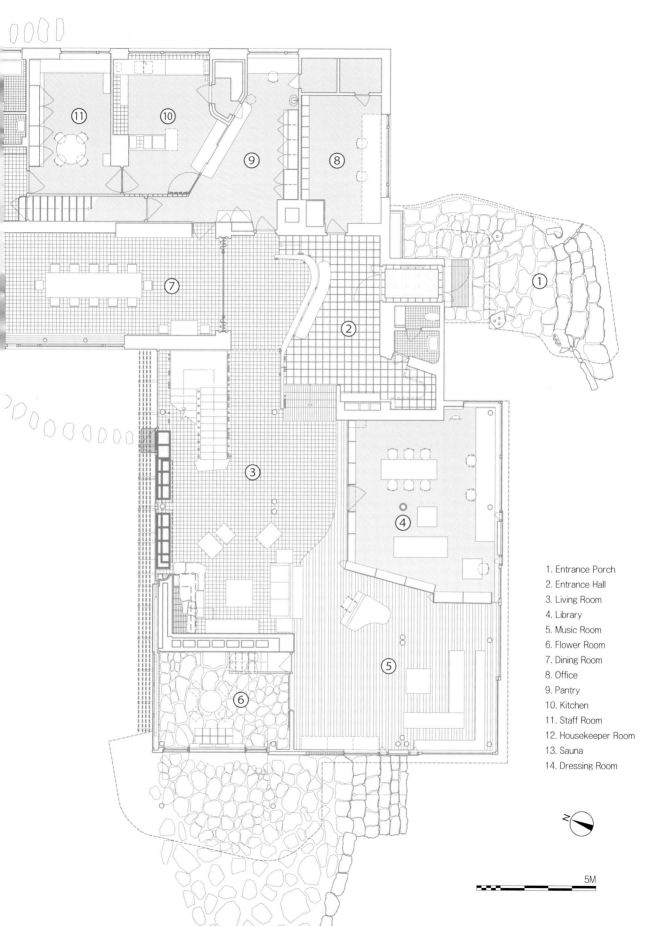

1. Entrance Porch
2. Entrance Hall
3. Living Room
4. Library
5. Music Room
6. Flower Room
7. Dining Room
8. Office
9. Pantry
10. Kitchen
11. Staff Room
12. Housekeeper Room
13. Sauna
14. Dressing Room

5M

冬の午後。リビングルームからミュージックルームを見る
Winter afternoon. The music room viewed from the living room.

丘の上に立つため、冬の朝日は水平に室内を貫通する
Morning sunlight penetrates horizontally into the room in winter.

書斎。天井はリビングエリアとひとつながりで、壁の上部を欄間でゆるやかに仕切る。手前のチェスはマックス・エルンストのデザイン、絵はピカソ

Library. Its ceiling is linked to the living area, with the upper part over the wall subtly divided by the transoms. The chessboard and chess pieces are designed by Max Ernst and the pictures are by Picasso.

ダイニングルーム。日没ぎりぎりまで林を縫って部屋に入射する西日。さりげないが絶妙な暖炉側の壁のプロポーション。傾斜をつけた天井や窓まわりのディテールワークは非の打ち所がない

Dining room. The afternoon sunlight slants in through the woods to the last minute of sunset. The proportions of the fireplace-side wall are simple but delicate. The effects of the slanting ceiling and details around the windows are exceptional.

北東の松林に向けて窓を開いたキッチン
Kitchen. It looks out to the pinewoods on the northeastern side.

ダイニングルームへつながる廊下からリビングルームを見る。柱間から見えるのはレジェ、カンディンスキー、ポリアコフ、正面はグリスの絵

The living room viewed from the corridor leading to the dining room. Visible through the columns and poles are paintings by Léger, Kandinsky, Poliakoff; the painting on the opposite wall is by Juan Gris.

（上）マイレ・グリクセンのベッドルーム
（左）２階の階段ホール。廊下に曲面の壁を立て、滑らかな空間移動の感覚をつくりだす

(Above) Maire Gullichsen's bedroom.
(Left) Upper hall. The curved wall keeps the traffic lines smooth in this space of intersecting human movement.

夏の屋根は白い小花で彩られる
The roof is decorated with small white flowers in summer.

伝統的なサウナはアールトの住宅に不可欠な要素
Traditional-style sauna is an indispensable element of Aalto's houses

この家では客のもてなしはサウナからはじまる
Entertainment of guests begins with the sauna in the villa.

中庭を囲んだＬ形の建物。午後から光がまわってくる
The L-shaped building encloses the courtyard. Sunlight enters here in the afternoon.

巧みな開閉バランス。煙突の垂直性が全体の印象を引き締める
Note the skillful balance of open and closed. The chimney's verticality injects a bracing tension to the design of the whole.

Villa Mairea

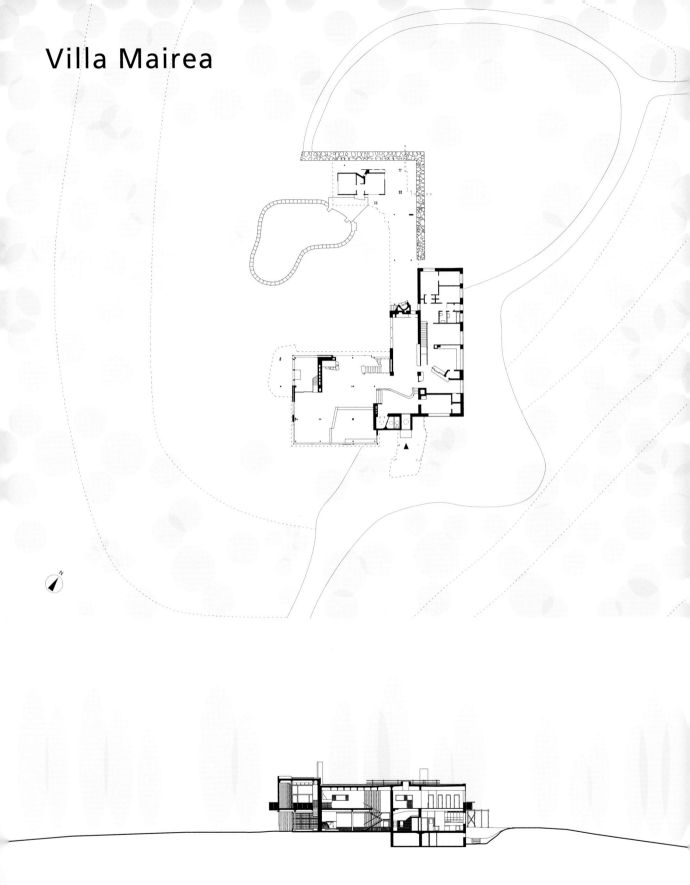

S 1:600

The Villa Mairea is in the village of Noormarkku in the suburbs of Finland's west coast port town of Pori, about 200 kilometers northwest of Helsinki. The area is the home of the Ahlström paper company. Maire Gullichsen, daughter of the company's owner, and her husband Harry Gullichsen, who succeeded to management of the company when young, asked Alvar Aalto and his wife, Aino, their close friends, to design their house.

Maire, after whom the house was named, aspired to spread avant-garde art in Finland after studying modern art in Paris under cubist painter Fernand Léger. Around that time, Alvar Aalto was expanding his personal connections with avant-garde artists, including Léger, László Moholy-Nagy, and Alexander Calder, with whom he became acquainted in the late 1920s.

Maire's husband, Harry Gullichsen, was a businessman of enterprising spirit. In 1936, in a venture project with other paper companies, he assigned Aalto to design the Sunila Pulp Mill in Kotka and prepare a master plan of the town. Maire and Harry Gullichsen were clients who had a decisive influence on Aalto's career both in terms of personal connections with modern artists and direct access to industrialists. When they requested him to design their house, Aalto was 39 and his wife 43, while Maire was 30 and Harry 35. Members of the same generation with the exuberant spirit of "comrades," they shared the aspiration to make society better from their respective positions.

The Villa Mairea stands at the top of a gentle hill rising to a height of about 20 meters, surrounded by red pine and birch forest in a rural landscape. Building a house on such an open hilltop, it made sense to first consider how to open the building to its natural surroundings. As Aalto's initial sketches indicate, however, he sought to enclose the house and insert within it a courtyard connecting daily life with outside. He also planned a pergola and a terrace within the courtyard. He created in-between spaces linking interior and exterior, and in those spaces introduced elements of fire and water as focal points where people would gather. This technique he was to employ later in the Säynätsalo Town Hall (1948–52), the National Pensions Institute (1948–57), and the Aalto Summer House (1952–53), among other designs.

The Villa Mairea is not entirely enclosed but built in an L-shape plan, with the major spaces of the living and dining rooms opened wide to the courtyard. The living room faces a sauna hut

スニラ製紙工場
Sunila Pulp Mill (1936–54).

ヘルシンキから北西へ200kmほど、西海岸の港町ポリ近郊のノールマルク村にこの住宅はある。この地域は製紙会社アールストローム社の発祥の地で、経営者の娘マイレ・グリクセンと、その夫で会社の経営を若くして引き継いだハリー・グリクセンが、1937年、親しい友人のアールト夫妻に住宅設計を依頼する。

　この家の名前の由来ともなったマイレは、パリでモダンアートを学び、フェルナン・レジェに師事、フィンランドに前衛芸術を広めたいと考えていた。一方アールトは、1930年代前半から出会ったレジェやモホリ・ナジ、カルダーをはじめとする前衛的なアーティストとの人脈を広げつつあった。

　他方、マイレの夫ハリー・グリクセンは進取の気性に富んだ実業家で、1936年、ほかの製紙会社とのヴェンチャー事業で、コトカにスニラ製紙工場の設計と町のマスタープランづくりをアールトに依頼している。グリクセン夫妻は、今後アールトが歩むキャリアに決定的な影響を及ぼす、二つの方向性を兼ね備えたクライアントだったのである。一つはモダンアート関係の人脈、もう一つは企業家との太いパイプである。アールトはこのとき39歳、妻のアイノが43歳、一方、マイレは30歳、ハリーは35歳で、同世代の意気軒昂な彼らは、それぞれの立場から社会をよりよいものにしようと大志を抱く「同胞」でもあった。

　敷地は、アカマツやカバの林に囲まれた美しい田園風景が広がるなか、20mほど起伏のついたなだらかな丘の上にある。このように恵まれた環境で、広々とした丘の上に家を建てるとなれば、いかに建築を自然に開放するかを考えるのが定石ではなかろうか。しかし、初期段階のスケッチが物語るように、アールトは囲って閉じ、そのなかに自然と生活とを取りもつ中庭をつくろうとする。さらには、中庭にパーゴラを設けたり、テラスをつくったりして、外と内との中間領域を必ずつくり、そこに人が集まるフォーカルポイントとなる火や水の要素を入れるのである。この手法は、のちのセイナッツァロの役場(1948−52)、国民年金会館(1948−57)、夏の家(1952−53)などでも使われている。

　ただし、閉じるといっても、ヴィラ・マイレアではコートハウスの「口の字形」ではなくL形プランにして、リビングやダイニングといった主要空間を中庭へ向けて大きく開いている。リビング正面向かい側には「離れ」となったサウナ小屋があり、母屋とサウナとはテラスでゆるやかに連結されている。このテラスには外暖炉が設けられ、サウナのあとに暖を取ったり、炉辺で食事が楽しめるようになっている。

　ところで、最初に敷地を見たとき、建物をどの方向へ向けて、どんな形にするか——アールトが

周囲の敷地環境
Idyllic setting.

across the courtyard, and the sauna and the main building are connected by a covered terrace. The terrace is equipped with an outdoor fireplace for keeping warm after using the sauna or during meals eaten out-of-doors.

When he first looked at a site, Aalto decided in which direction the building would face and what shape it would take according to the direction of the sun, the configuration of the land, and the views from the site. His sketches often include arrows resulting from his study of these factors. Several initial sketches for the Villa Mairea showing such arrows have been preserved. These sketches show that Aalto's basic approach to the house was to create a courtyard upon which the building would throw no shadow from noon onward. In the Villa Mairea one can enjoy the shifting sunlight from sunrise to sunset. Rather than creating rooms into which sunlight enters throughout the day, Aalto planned each room so that it would receive sunlight during the time most suitable to the room.

The entrance hall, the library, and the music room on the first floor and the bedrooms on the second floor are arranged from the eastern to southern sides in order to receive morning sunlight. The dining room, on the other hand, faces west, allowing enjoyment of the setting sun to the last minute during the evening meal. On the north side, which receives afternoon sunlight, is the sauna hut made of wood. From the living room, which faces the hut across the courtyard, one can see the sauna shining in the rays of the descending sun.

The concept of this house being fusion between modern art and daily living, Aalto was called upon to create a totally new quality of living space. He struggled hard to realize this demand. He agonized most over the program for mingling art and daily life. Aalto considered a number of possibilities such as building a gallery as an annex within the site or making a gallery space in the house, but he finally arrived at a concept of a "plain single room," that is, a smooth, continuous single space from the entrance hall, to the living room, and then to the library, partitioned only by movable walls. He proposed, moreover, that shelves be made within the walls that partitioned the spaces to store art works and that pictures be hung on the outside of the walls. "In this way," he wrote, "it is easy for the host or hostess to work with the collection, to take out the pictures, place them on the wall, and change them again."[12]

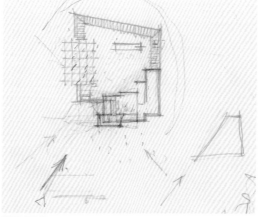

敷地のスタディ
Site plan study.

決め手とするのは、太陽の方位、土地の形状、周囲の眺めであり、スケッチにはそれをスタディした矢印を描きこんだものが多い。つまり、矢印は方位や視界を示している。ヴィラ・マイレアの初期のスケッチにも矢印の描かれたものが何枚か残されているが、そこからわかるのは、アールトのこの住宅への根本的な考えは、正午以降、建物の影にならない中庭をつくることである。ヴィラ・マイレアは朝日から夕日まで、絶え間なく変化に富んだ光を楽しめる家だが、アールトは一日中光が入ってくる部屋をつくるというよりは、各部屋にいちばん適した時間帯の光を入れるべくプランを組みたてる。まず、1階では玄関ホール、書斎、ミュージックルーム、2階では寝室群を東側から南側へ配置し、午前中の光が各部屋に入るようにしている。一方、ダイニングルームは夕日をぎりぎりまで楽しみながら食事ができるよう、西に向けられている。北側には木造のサウナ小屋を配置しているが、午後からの光がこの建物にあたる。その対面にあるリビングルームから、西日に照らされるサウナを眺められる構成である。

　この住宅のコンセプトは、モダンアートと生活が融合する家をつくることであり、アールトはこれまでにない新しい住空間の答を出すよう求められ、それを何とか具現化しようと悪戦苦闘した。いちばん頭を悩ませたのは、アートと生活の共存をはかるためのプログラムづくりだった。アールトは敷地のなかにギャラリーを別棟にして建てるのを考えたり、家のなかにギャラリースペースをつくるのを検討したりするが、最後の最後に、「飾り気のないワンルーム」というコンセプトにたどりつく。つまり、玄関ホールからはじまって、リビングルームから書斎、ミュージックルームまで、ゆるやかに仕切りつつ、滑らかに連続するシングルスペースの構成である。さらには、その空間を仕切る壁のなかを美術品の収蔵庫とし、壁の外側に絵を掛けるのを提案する。「こうすれば、家のあるじは自分のコレクションと楽につきあえます。絵を取りだしては掛け、時々それを変えればよいのです」[12]と語っている。

　アールトはこの頃、日本の建築や文化に強い関心を抱いており、状況に応じて美術品の展示を変える着想については、日本の住空間の「しつらい」からヒントを得たものである。四季折々の花や掛け軸を一つだけ選び、床の間に飾る考え方である。ほかにも、ヴィラ・マイレアでは日本の影響が随所に反映されているが、各部屋にフレキシブルなパーティションをつけ、それを開け放てば一室空間となる構成は、日本古来からの空間のあり方そのものである。さらには、内部空間から外部空間への連続性である。これは初期からアールトのテーマではあったが、この住宅ではその意識はさらに明確で、庭との一体感が強く求められている。じつは、リビングルームの大きなガラス面は

絵の収蔵庫も兼ねた仕切り壁。彫刻はジャン・アルプ
Partition wall serving as storage for paintings. Sculpture by Jean Arp.

Around that time, Aalto had a strong interest in Japanese architecture and culture, and his idea of changing art works on display anytime came from the Japanese practice of *shitsurai* ("decorating the room") by which flowers and a hanging scroll are chosen and displayed in the tokonoma alcove in accordance with the cycle of the seasons. Japanese influences are reflected in many other places in the Villa Mairea. For example, each room has flexible partitions, removal of which unites adjacent spaces. This approach to the composition of space has a long tradition in Japanese architecture since ancient times. Also, continuity between interior and exterior space, another Japanese feature, was one of Aalto's themes from early in his career. His pursuit of this continuity is clear at the Villa Mairea, where emphasis is given to unity with the courtyard. The large windows of the living room are moveable and when opened completely leave only the pillars. The interior space joins with that of the courtyard, blending the air of interior and exterior.

A highlight of this house is the glimpses afforded through intervening columns of the living area and courtyard beyond as soon as one comes into the entrance hall. Another feature is the sense of smooth physical movement as one climbs the four steps leading from the entrance hall and the living room comes gradually come into full view. The scene that unfolds above the steps is the most dramatic in the Villa Mairea. Aalto skillfully placed an invisible diagonal line of vision in that main space. He inserted a curving white wall in the entrance hall and guides the line of vision along the wall deeper and deeper diagonally until it reaches the living room fireplace and the painting of a guitar (by Juan Gris) hung on the limewashed white brick wall. In the center of the living room, moreover, is the rattan-wrapped double column. No matter from which direction you look, this column is always in your range of vision, adding depth to the perception of the space.

The details are faultless: the ceiling in the first floor main space covered with slender closely fit pine slats, the smooth sequence of different flooring materials, the white walls around the fireplace with their rough and smooth textures of plaster, to name a few. The composition of space, and the technical virtuosity in the expression of every element—the Villa Mairea, with all aspects of it harmonizing in a perfected order, is certainly one of Aalto's best works.

玄関ホールからの眺め
View from the entrance hall.

可動式になっており、全開にすれば柱だけが残る。そのとき内部と庭とは滑らかに連なり、互いの空気は融けあうのである。

　この住宅のハイライトは、玄関ホールにたたずんだとき、林立する柱を透かして奥に感じられるリビングエリアや庭の気配であり、さらには、4段の階段を上りつつ視界に入ってくるリビングルーム、そのときの滑らかな身体の動きである。階段の先に広がる光景がヴィラ・マイレアの見せ場である。アールトが巧みなのは、このメインスペースに「見えない斜めの視線」を仕組んだ点だ。湾曲した白い壁を玄関ホールに挿入し、それに沿わせるようにして人の視線を斜め方向に奥へと引っ張っている。それを受けとめるのが暖炉であり、石灰塗りレンガの白壁に掛かるギターの絵（フアン・グリス）である。さらに、リビングルームの中央には藤を巻いた二本柱を立て、この柱がどの方向から見ても視界に入ることで、空間の奥行が増幅されている。

　ディテールは非の打ち所がない。たとえば、マツの細板を張りあわせた天井、フローリング素材の滑らかな切り替え、白漆喰をラフなテクスチャーとスベスベのテクスチャーに塗りわけた暖炉まわりの壁など、枚挙にいとまがない。空間構成、ディテールワーク、一つ一つのエレメントの表現方法——ヴィラ・マイレアはすべてが高い秩序のなかで調和した、アールトの最高傑作である。

冬の朝日
Morning light in winter.

ランドスケープ、プラン、エレベーションのスタディ
Landscape, plan, and elevation study.

著者紹介

齋藤 裕 建築家

1947 北海道小樽市生まれ
     独学で建築を学ぶ
1970 齋藤裕建築研究所を設立
1986 日本建築家協会新人賞を「るるるる阿房」で受賞
1992 吉田五十八賞を「好日居」で受賞
1993 東京アートディレクターズクラブ・原弘賞を『ルイス・バラガンの建築』で受賞
1998 日本建築学会・北海道建築賞を「曼月居」で受賞
2000 日本建築学会・学会賞および作品選奨を「曼月居」で受賞

建築作品集に、『齋藤裕の建築』（1998 年／ TOTO 出版）、
『現代の建築家シリーズ 齋藤裕』（1994 年／鹿島出版会）がある。
また、近年は写真を媒介として空間を探求する試みをはじめ、
写真集に、『ルイス・バラガンの建築』（1992 年／ TOTO 出版・1994 年／メキシコ・ノリエガ出版、
改訂版：1996 年／ TOTO 出版）、
『フェリックス・キャンデラの世界』（1995 年／ TOTO 出版）、
『建築の詩人 カルロ・スカルパ』（1997 年／ TOTO 出版）、
『カーサ・バラガン』（2002 年／ TOTO 出版）、
『ルイス・カーンの全住宅』（2003 年／ TOTO 出版）、
『ヴィラ・マイレア／アルヴァ・アールト』（2005 年／ TOTO 出版）がある。
そのほかに、エッセイ集『STRONG』（1991 年／住まいの図書館出版局）、
『建築のエッセンス』（2000 年／ A. D. A. EDITA Tokyo）が出版されている。

Author

Yutaka Saito Architect

1947	Born in Otaru City, Hokkaido, Japan.
	Studied architecture independently.
1970	Founded Yutaka Saito Architect & Associates.
1986	Won the Japan Institute of Architects Prize for the work "Rurururu-abo."
1992	Won the Isoya Yoshida Memorial Prize for the work "Kojitsu-kyo."
1993	Won the Tokyo Art Directors Club Hiromu Hara Prize for *Luis Barragan*.
1998	Won the Hokkaido Architectural Prize of the Architectural Institute of Japan for "Mangetsu-kyo."
2000	Won the Architectural Institute of Japan Award for the work "Mangetsu-kyo."
	Won the 2000 Selected Architectural Design Award of the Architectural Institute of Japan for "Mangetsu-kyo."

Along with his architectural practice, he has begun to photograph architecture as part of his study of space and published photographic books as follows.

Luis Barragan (TOTO Publishing, Japan, 1992; Noriega Editores, Mexico, 1994),

Felix Candela (TOTO Publishing, 1995),

Carlo Scarpa (TOTO Publishing, 1997),

Casa Barragan (TOTO Publishing, 2002),

Louis I. Kahn Houses (TOTO Publishing, 2003), and

Villa Mairea/Alvar Aalto (TOTO Publishing, 2005).

The collection of his architectural works has been published in two books:

Gendai no kenchikuka shirizu Saito Yutaka [Contemporary Architect: Yutaka Saito] (Kajima Shuppankai, Japan, 1994) and *Yutaka Saito: Architect* (TOTO Publishing, Japan 1998).

Notes

1. Göran Schildt, *Inhimillinen tekijä: Alvar Aalto 1939−1976*. Keuruu: Otava Publishing Company, 1989.
Published in English as: *Alvar Aalto: The Mature Years*. Timothy Binham, trans. New York: Rizzoli International Publications, 1991, p. 233.
邦訳：『白い机―円熟期：アルヴァ・アアルトの栄光と憂うつ』田中雅美・田中智子共訳、鹿島出版会、1998 年

2. Göran Schildt. *Valkoinen pöytä: Alvar Aallon nuoruus ja taiteelliset perusideat*. Keuruu: Otava Publishing Company, 1982.
Published in English as: *Alvar Aalto: The Early Years*. Timothy Binham, trans. New York: Rizzoli International Publications, 1984.
邦訳：『白い机―若い時：アルヴァ・アアルトの青年時代と芸術思想』田中雅美・田中智子共訳、鹿島出版会、1989 年

3. Originally published in *Casabella Continuità*, March, 1954. Republished in *Alvar Aalto in His Own Words*, Göran Schildt, ed., Timothy Binham, trans. Keuruu: Otava Publishing Company, 1997, p. 38.

4. Göran Schildt. *Inhimillinen tekijä: Alvar Aalto 1939−1976*. Keuruu: Otava Publishing Company, 1989.
Published in English as: *Alvar Aalto: The Mature Years*. Timothy Binham, trans. New York: Rizzoli International Publications, 1991, p. 158.

5. Markku Lahti, *Alvar Aalto Houses*. Helsinki: Rakennustieto Oy, 2005, p. 128.

6. Markku Lahti. "Alvar Aalto's One-family Houses: Paradises for Ordinary People," *a+u* (Extra edition, June 1998). Tokyo: A+U Publishing Co., p. 6.
マルック・ラティ：「アルヴァ・アアルトの住宅：普通の人々のためのパラダイス」『建築と都市』(1998 年 6 月臨時増刊号) エー・アンド・ユー、p. 15

7. Yutaka Saito. "The Villa as an Experiment for Aalto: Interview with Kristian Gullichsen," *Alvar Aalto/Villa Mairea*. Tokyo: TOTO Shuppan, 2005, p. 190.
齋藤裕：クリスチャン・グリクセン・インタビュー「この住宅は、アールトにとって実験だったのです」『ヴィラ・マイレア／アルヴァ・アールト』TOTO 出版、2005 年、p. 191

8. Sirkkaliisa Jetsonen. "Close-ups: A World of Materials and Details," *Alvar Aalto Houses*. Helsinki: Rakennustieto Oy, 2005, p. 10.

9. Göran Schildt. *Alvar Aalto: The Complete Catalogue of Architecture, Design and Art*. New York: Rizzoli International Publications, 1994, pp. 314-317.

10. *Alvar Aalto Houses*, p.128.

11. Originally published in the sample issue of *Aitta* magazine, 1926. Republished in *Alvar Aalto in His Own Words*. Göran Schildt, ed., Timothy Binham, trans., Keuruu: Otava Publishing Company, 1997, pp. 50-55.

12. From a lecture given at Yale University, May 9, 1939. Reprinted in *Alvar Aalto in His Own Words*. Göran Schildt, ed., Timothy Binham, trans., Keuruu: Otava Publishing Company, 1997, p. 228.

Illustration Credits

Photographs by Yutaka Saito except the mentioned below.

©Alvar Aalto Foundation/Alvar Aalto Museum: Drawings and Photographical Collection
p. 15: photo by Gōran Schildt, pp. 36-37: 84-1464, pp. 38-39: 84-1444, 84-1447, pp. 40-41: 84-1270, 84-1280, pp. 50-51: 84-1613, p. 60: 84-1353, p. 61: 84-1414, pp. 74-75: 84-1670, p. 79: 101915, photo by Heikki Havas, pp. 82-83: 84-1609, p. 91: 101911 photo by Heikki Havas, p. 92: 101859 photo by Heikki Havas, p. 93: 101896 photo by Heikki Havas, p. 94: 101907 photo by Heikki Havas, p. 95: 102092 photo by Heikki Havas, p. 96: Iittala Eskimo1, photo by Hackman Pro Design Foundation/ Iittala Glass Museum, Iittala, p. 99 Pavia, p. 100: Marl5, p. 101: 84-1270, p. 105: 86-299, p. 130: 84-71 p. 131: 84-70, p. 147: L-414 photo by Martti Kapanen, p. 148: 84-67, p. 151: 84-003-136 photo by Wolfgang Heine, p. 172: 86-299, p. 173: 86-358 (top), 86-355 (bottom), p. 178: 86-383, p. 179: 86-382, p. 185: 100349 photo by Federico Marconi, p. 195: 86-423, p. 201: 86-425, pp. 208-209: 84-1970, pp. 220-221: 84-1973 (top), 84-1974 (bottom), pp. 224-225: 84-1936 (top), 84-1972 (bottom), p. 235: 84-1900, p. 242: 80-832, p. 261: 80-873, p. 268: 84-1779, p. 272: 84-1769, p. 281, pp. 288-289, p. 296, p. 297, p. 300, p. 304, p. 311, p. 321: 84-45, p. 326: 84-30 (left), 84-32 (right), p. 383: 84-268, p. 387: 84-164

Acknowledgements

We would like to express our profound gratitude to Alvar Aalto Museum and Alvar Aalto Foundation for their generous support.
Also, we are deeply grateful for the cooperation of the house owners and the persons involved in the administration of Aalto works as follows.

Villa Mairea
Kristian Gullichsen, Kirsi Gullichsen, Anna Hall

Maison Carré
Markku Lahti, Ásdis Ólafsdóttir, Yann Guillard

Villa Schildt
Göran Schildt, Christine Schildt

Aalto House & Studio
Ulla Kinnunen

Aalto Summer House
Alvar Aalto Musuem

Enso Gutzeit (Stora Enso)
Juha Mäkimattila

Maison Aho
Pekka Pälsynaho, Ari Aho

Villa Kokkonen
City of Järvenpää, Salminen Jari, Helena Rummukainen

Villa Oksala
Markku Lahti

Villa Tammekann
Pekka Kanervisto

Sunila Pulp Mill
Rurik Wasastjerna

翻訳　Translation
リン・E・リッグス　Lynne E. Riggs
武智学　Manabu Takechi

図面制作　Drawing
丸谷晴道　Harumichi Maruya
小篠隆生＋北海道大学大学院工学研究科有志
（青木潤・石田準・猪股悠・丸山和基：主要作品プラン）
Takao Ozasa & his students of the Graduate School of Engineering, Hokkaido University
得能一弥（ヴィラ・マイレア実測図）Kazuya Tokunoh (Measured Drawing of Villa Mairea)

AALTO: 10 Selected Houses
アールトの住宅

2008年3月31日 初版第1刷発行
2021年9月30日 初版第7刷発行

著・写真　　　齋藤 裕
発行者　　　　伊藤剛士
発行所　　　　TOTO出版 (TOTO株式会社)
〒107-0062　東京都港区南青山1-24-3
TOTO乃木坂ビル2F
[営業] TEL: (03) 3402-7138 FAX: (03) 3402-7187
[編集] TEL: (03) 3497-1010
URL: https://jp.toto.com/publishing
編集　　　　　三輪直美
デザイン　　　小島良平・小島良太
印刷・製本　　図書印刷株式会社

Printed in Japan
ISBN978-4-88706-290-0

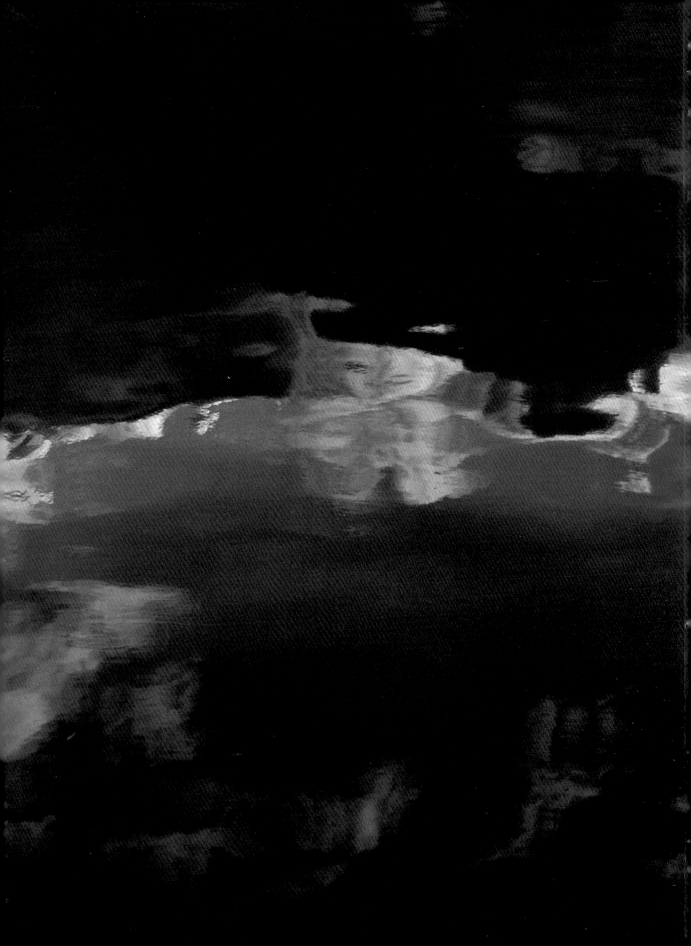